Sermons for children; being a course of fifty-two, on subjects suited to their tender age, and in a style adapted to the understanding of the rising generation: ... by the Reverend Mark Anthony Meilan. In three volumes. ... Volume 2 of 3

Mark Anthony Meilan

ECCO
PRINT EDITIONS

Sermons for children; being a course of fifty-two, on subjects suited to their tender age, and in a style adapted to the understanding of the rising generation: ... by the Reverend Mark Anthony Meilan. In three volumes. ... Volume 2 of 3

Meilan, Mark Anthony
ESTCID: T124423
Reproduction from British Library
With a list of subscribers at the end of vol. 3.
London : printed for T. Hookham, and T. Longman, 1789.
3v. ; 12°

Eighteenth Century
Collections Online
Print Editions

Gale ECCO Print Editions

Relive history with *Eighteenth Century Collections Online*, now available in print for the independent historian and collector. This series includes the most significant English-language and foreign-language works printed in Great Britain during the eighteenth century, and is organized in seven different subject areas including literature and language; medicine, science, and technology; and religion and philosophy. The collection also includes thousands of important works from the Americas.

The eighteenth century has been called "The Age of Enlightenment." It was a period of rapid advance in print culture and publishing, in world exploration, and in the rapid growth of science and technology – all of which had a profound impact on the political and cultural landscape. At the end of the century the American Revolution, French Revolution and Industrial Revolution, perhaps three of the most significant events in modern history, set in motion developments that eventually dominated world political, economic, and social life.

In a groundbreaking effort, Gale initiated a revolution of its own: digitization of epic proportions to preserve these invaluable works in the largest online archive of its kind. Contributions from major world libraries constitute over 175,000 original printed works. Scanned images of the actual pages, rather than transcriptions, recreate the works *as they first appeared.*

Now for the first time, these high-quality digital scans of original works are available via print-on-demand, making them readily accessible to libraries, students, independent scholars, and readers of all ages.

For our initial release we have created seven robust collections to form one the world's most comprehensive catalogs of 18th century works.

Initial Gale ECCO Print Editions collections include:

History and Geography

Rich in titles on English life and social history, this collection spans the world as it was known to eighteenth-century historians and explorers. Titles include a wealth of travel accounts and diaries, histories of nations from throughout the world, and maps and charts of a world that was still being discovered. Students of the War of American Independence will find fascinating accounts from the British side of conflict.

Social Science
Delve into what it was like to live during the eighteenth century by reading the first-hand accounts of everyday people, including city dwellers and farmers, businessmen and bankers, artisans and merchants, artists and their patrons, politicians and their constituents. Original texts make the American, French, and Industrial revolutions vividly contemporary.

Medicine, Science and Technology
Medical theory and practice of the 1700s developed rapidly, as is evidenced by the extensive collection, which includes descriptions of diseases, their conditions, and treatments. Books on science and technology, agriculture, military technology, natural philosophy, even cookbooks, are all contained here.

Literature and Language
Western literary study flows out of eighteenth-century works by Alexander Pope, Daniel Defoe, Henry Fielding, Frances Burney, Denis Diderot, Johann Gottfried Herder, Johann Wolfgang von Goethe, and others. Experience the birth of the modern novel, or compare the development of language using dictionaries and grammar discourses.

Religion and Philosophy
The Age of Enlightenment profoundly enriched religious and philosophical understanding and continues to influence present-day thinking. Works collected here include masterpieces by David Hume, Immanuel Kant, and Jean-Jacques Rousseau, as well as religious sermons and moral debates on the issues of the day, such as the slave trade. The Age of Reason saw conflict between Protestantism and Catholicism transformed into one between faith and logic -- a debate that continues in the twenty-first century.

Law and Reference
This collection reveals the history of English common law and Empire law in a vastly changing world of British expansion. Dominating the legal field is the *Commentaries of the Law of England* by Sir William Blackstone, which first appeared in 1765. Reference works such as almanacs and catalogues continue to educate us by revealing the day-to-day workings of society.

Fine Arts
The eighteenth-century fascination with Greek and Roman antiquity followed the systematic excavation of the ruins at Pompeii and Herculaneum in southern Italy; and after 1750 a neoclassical style dominated all artistic fields. The titles here trace developments in mostly English-language works on painting, sculpture, architecture, music, theater, and other disciplines. Instructional works on musical instruments, catalogs of art objects, comic operas, and more are also included.

The BiblioLife Network

This project was made possible in part by the BiblioLife Network (BLN), a project aimed at addressing some of the huge challenges facing book preservationists around the world. The BLN includes libraries, library networks, archives, subject matter experts, online communities and library service providers. We believe every book ever published should be available as a high-quality print reproduction; printed on-demand anywhere in the world. This insures the ongoing accessibility of the content and helps generate sustainable revenue for the libraries and organizations that work to preserve these important materials.

GUIDE TO FOLD-OUTS MAPS and OVERSIZED IMAGES

The book you are reading was digitized from microfilm captured over the past thirty to forty years. Years after the creation of the original microfilm, the book was converted to digital files and made available in an online database.

In an online database, page images do not need to conform to the size restrictions found in a printed book. When converting these images back into a printed bound book, the page sizes are standardized in ways that maintain the detail of the original. For large images, such as fold-out maps, the original page image is split into two or more pages

Guidelines used to determine how to split the page image follows:

• Some images are split vertically; large images require vertical and horizontal splits.
• For horizontal splits, the content is split left to right.
• For vertical splits, the content is split from top to bottom.
• For both vertical and horizontal splits, the image is processed from top left to bottom right.

SERMONS.

SERMONS

FOR
CHILDREN;

BEING A COURSE OF FIFTY-TWO,

ON

SUBJECTS

SUITED TO THEIR TENDER AGE, AND IN A STYLE
ADAPTED TO THE UNDERSTANDING OF

THE RISING GENERATION:

BEING AN ATTEMPT

TO COUNSEL AND IMPROVE THE HEART, BY
OCCUPYING THE IMAGINATION.

WITH A HYMN ANNEXED TO EACH DISCOURSE.

THE WHOLE

By the Reverend *MARK ANTHONY MEILAN.*

IN THREE VOLUMES.

VOL. II.

DELIGHTFUL TASK!
THOMPSON'S SEASONS.

LONDON:

PRINTED FOR T HOOKHAM, IN NEW BOND-STREET,
AND T. LONGMAN, PATER-NOSTER-ROW.
MDCCLXXXIX.

CONTENTS.

SERMONS for CHILDREN.

SERMON XVII.

ON EASTER DAY.

ROMANS iv. v. 25.

—And was raised again for our Justification.

OUR Lord was crucified upon a Friday, which we therefore call *Good Friday*, using, very possibly, a name too homely for the purpose such a day promotes. From Friday to the Sunday, when he rose, including both, are three: hence, therefore, that expression in our creed, *was crucified, was dead and buried; he descended into hell, and on the third day rose again.*

In the preceding sermon we informed you, that the Jewish priests and council, thinking Jesus a deceiver, if they really did think so, and procuring, by their interest with Pilate, who was procurator of Judea, firſt, his condemnation to a cruel death; and ſecondly, his execution for infringing on the rights of Cæſai, though his crime, in their idea, was pretending to be God's own Son, had placed a guard about his tomb, becauſe when they had gone thus far, it was their intereſt to prevent his friends conſpiring to bear off the body fiom the ſepulchre, and then give out that he was riſen from the dead, which riſing, he had always ſaid, would be the caſe,

This guard, we muſt ſuppoſe, were well acquainted with their duty. They were ſoldiers, and at leaſt would keep ſuch watch, that the diſciples, one of whom had openly denied his maſter, and the reſt forſaken him, that the diſciples, we repeat, a helpleſs, deſtitute, and friendleſs company of men, and ſuch as had no greater influence than at preſent we may think a band of fiſhermen might have, ſhould not preſume to undertake the dangerous taſk of breaking open their redeemer's tomb, and ſtealing him away. Among the Jews and Romans it was no light matter to diſturb the ſacred manſions of the dead, and therefore was the puniſhment of thoſe, who durſt attempt it. a ſevere one : ſo too, for a ſoldier to keep watch in such a manner, that the very thing he was appointed to prevent, should, notwithstanding all his vigilance be brought about, would have excited great suspicion in the breast of his superiors. These particulars we introduce, dear little friends, since, notwithstanding the impossibility that any soldiers who were placed about the tomb of Christ, to awe his friends, and keep them from the act of carrying off his body, should keep watch so negligently that the body, after all, should really be carried off, and notwithstanding the improbability that his disciples should conceive so mad a project, the report of those appointed to keep watch was this: that on the third day after they were set, this project was attempted with success while they were sleeping.

We have dwelt upon this matter rather fully, little friends, because if in your tender age we can persuade you that the Saviour really did rise again, we shall go very far in making you hereafter real Christians, such as will not, as St. Paul expresses it, be blown about by every blast of doctrine: since, if once the resurrection of Christ Jesus is but proved, the wonder of his birth, which is not sure a greater miracle, will need no proof. We say then, that if Jesus

Christ

Chrift did not miraculoufly rife again from death, he muft, as faid the guard, have privately been ftolen from the fepulchre, and *that* by his difciples: but it is not likely, that if, after the redeemer's crucifixion, they had once difcovered from his inability to rife again, as he he had promifed them would be the cafe, he had been nothing more than a deceiver, they would then have been fo fteadfaft in the faith he taught them, and expofed their perfons to the rifque of death, with torture, for the fake of an impoftor. Men are not fo fond of being duped as that amounts to.

Therefore he *did* rife again, for on the day which, by the Jewifh method of computing time, begins their week, *that* Mary, who was called Magdalene, with John and Peter, ignorant that any refurrection of their lord had taken place, came early to the fepulchre. The woman firft arrived, and found it open, neither did fhe fee the foldiers, who were all gone off. She, coming back, told John and Peter, who ran forward, and, both going in, were fure that Jefus Chrift was rifen. Upon this they went their way, but Mary ftaid behind, and weeping, ftooped to look into the tomb, when lo! fhe faw two angels cloathed in white, and

fitting

fitting where had been the head and feet of
Jefus. They enquired the reafon of her tears,
and fhe had fcarce replied, when happening to
turn round, fhe faw the Saviour ftanding, whofe
firft words we need not mention. He con-
cluded his difcourfe by bidding her go tell his
brethren, as he called them, meaning the difciples, he was rifen, which fhe did; and on the
evening of that day, when the difciples were
affembled, but in private, as they feared the
Jews, came Jefus, faying: *Peace be to you.*

After this he parted from them, and a fecond
time appeared to fome of his difciples, who
were fifhing in the fea. as foon as he ap-
proached them, he was known by the fur-
prizing quantity of fifh they caught. And here
to fhew them that his body, made up as it
was of flefh and bones, had rifen from the
dead, and not his fpirit only, he eat with them,
which a fpirit cannot do.

And thus, dear little friends, in this, and the
preceding two difcourfes, have we drawn you
out a brief narration of the life, the death, and
refurrection of Chrift Jefus, reckoning from
the period he was born at Bethlehem. We are
now to fill up the remaining part of this difcourfe with fome account, although a brief

B 3 one,

one, of the moral taught us by the life, the
death, and refurrection of Chrift Jefus : for no
action, as already we have faid, was he con-
cerned in that did not convey fome leffon of
inftruction to mankind ; among which number
you are likewife comprehended.

In a word then, the redeemer's life affords
you many fhining inftances of that humility,
that charity, and refignation to God's will,
which every one among us fhould take caie to
imitate : his death is in itfelf a type or fymbol
of that death to fin, which we fhould all experience.   Thefe two points, in many places,
we have fpoken of already ; and his refurrection is a token of that birth to righteoufnefs we
ought to be renewed with.   You, good little
ones, are in that ftage of life, which, though
it knows no actual righteoufnefs, has all the
confequences of imputed righteoufnefs.   A time
will come, if providence fhould fo long fpare
you, when that righteoufnefs, from which alone
you can draw any merit, muft be manifefted in
your works : then, for your comfort, you may
recollect what you are told at prefent , that the
refurrection of Chrift Jefus, if you turn it to
the ufe for which it was intended, will fupply

you

you with a newnefs firft of life ; and fecondly, of reafon.

With a newnefs firft of life : for fure without much obfervation, looking at yourfelves, and contemplating that fmooth countenance peculiar to your time of life, and afterwards confidering thofe deep furrows to be noticed in the countenance of others, who were once what you are now ; you may with eafe convince yourfelves that in the womb of nature, or your mothers', you received that principle of mutability, or change, which will, at one time or another, make you what they are, and afterwards deftroy you, that in future all that cheerfulnefs of countenance, and all that pliancy of limb, which makes you now fo lively, will be turned into a thoughtfulnefs of brow, and indolence of difpofition: and ftill more, that in the womb, you entered as it were into a fpecies of apprenticefhip with death : but this we fay by no means to dejeſt your tender bofoms. You will hear us fpeaking in this manner, with as much indifference as you gaze at prefent on a funeral, as it paffes: and why fo? becaufe you are at prefent innocent. Keep then this innocence, and when hereafter you are come to years of underftanding, and are

talked

talked to of mortality, you will not liften with indifference then, but neither will your fpirit be depreffed at the idea of your tranfient nature but with Job you will be taught, by infpiration as it were, to place your hopes, not like the reft of men, on life, which is fo fhort, but on that death which is to introduce you to a never ending ftate of immortality, where you fhall have no reafon to exclaim, as he did in this ftate of being, " I muft look upon corruption as " my father, and the worm as if it were my " mother and my fifter."

Are you puzzled then at the idea of a refurrec-tion, fuch as the redeemer's was a type of; and already, though you are not ufed to argue but believe, do you begin to doubt there can be fuch a thing? If fo,—not to detain you with remarks upon yourfelves, and that continual change you are incurring, not to mention that among you there are fome, who would at prefent fcorn thofe little fports and paftimes which rejoiced your childhood, and afpire at greater pleafures now than heretofore you did; and will hereafter wifh for greater than what now content you, till the whole collected pleafures of this life will have no charms to entertain you and thofe appertaining to another

life

life alone be proper to engage your contemplation,—not, dear children, to detain you with thefe obfervations, which have no authority, becaufe adduced by one, who, notwithftanding he may be poffeffed of great affection for you, is an individual of no confequence: we fhall bring forward in this place the arguments St. Paul made ufe of on this fubject, and which arguments, you may remember, are in general read at burials. Being put into a drefs adapted to your juvenile or inexperienced underftanding, they are thefe. All creatures die, and others come into their place inceffantly. Your lovely youth, dear little company, has fprung from the decaying ftrength which many of you may obferve already in your parents. Go, and take a view, even though it be a fhort one, of your garden· all the flowers with which you are fo much delighted, fade and blow again fuccef-fively: the leaves fall off in autumn, and next fpring fhoot out again. Should you but put a grain of wheat into the ground, you would dif-cern it dies, as the apoftle tells us, or corrupts, before a ftalk appears, with wheat upon it; and when once you have attained the power of making fuitable reflections upon what you meet with, you will find that nature lofes no-

thing

thing, but that even death itſelf produces life. Why, therefore, aſks the apoſtle, cannot the Almighty do with man as with a grain of wheat? He will do ſo, good little friends, and at the end of all things, raiſe us up to that new life, of which the Saviour's is a type.

But ſecondly; the reſurrection of Chriſt Jeſus, if you turn it to the uſe for which it was intended, will ſupply you with a newneſs, as we ſaid before, of reaſon.

To diſcuſs this point of doctrine, we would turn your obſervation on the reaſon you poſſeſs already; which, though tender, is ſtill reaſon. What then is this reaſon through life's ſeveral ſtages? In the ſeaſon of your infancy, it is but blooming; in the time of your maturity, it is diſturbed by paſſion; in the ſtate of your old age, it is decaying. In the time of your maturity alone, when every faculty is vigorous with the body, it deſerves the name of reaſon, and is competent to weigh or balance circumſtances, and conduct the actions of your life by truth, and what philoſophers call moral fitneſs. But, as juſt now we obſerved, the paſſions bring it under their ſubjection. Of theſe paſſions, you as yet know hardly any thing: but ſtill, the little reaſon you poſſeſs is warped by

the

the imagination; and the power of this imagination, working upon reafon, is experienced
not by grown-up people only, as we call them,
but by children of the tendereft underftanding
likewife. Of this influence of imagination,
thus fuperior to the force of reafon, in the
minds of children, we are puzzled to adduce
you inftances. Some we could cite indeed,
but not of fuch a nature as to prove authorities.
Judge then, with what degree of force imagination works on reafon, by its wonderful effects,
in thofe of ripe or perfect underftanding. Some
among you may have read the Roman hiftory:
the death of Julius Cæfar in the fenate, brought
about by *Brutus* and his party, was a matter of
indifference to the people; but his robe, when
Antony difplayed it publickly, pierced through
and through by the confpirators, excited them
to vengeance. Is not this example of the
weaknefs of man's reafoning faculties fufficient? If it be not, we muft let you have
another. You have all then read the Bible.
David's murder of Uriah was a very trifle in
his eftimation: but the rich man's conduct,
who, as Nathan told him, had purloined or
ftolen his poor neighbour's lamb, that he
might entertain his gueft, was fo enormous an

B 6   offence

offence, that he protested by the Lord, he would
most surely put to death the man that had been
guilty of so black a crime.   Then likewise, is
your reasoning faculty affected by your make
and constitution: and even custom is a tyrant
that controuls it.   Hence that proverb, *Custom
is a second nature.*   Reason, therefore, such as
we enjoy at present, is at best no more than a
fallacious guide. but it will be perfectionated
during that new life of which the Saviour's resurrection is a symbol.

Thus, does that great festival, at present celebrated by the church, instruct you.   May you
all draw profit from the instruction. We desire
not that the Saviour's resurrection may restore
you from the dead, to mingle with the living.
but we pray that, as the text expresses it, you
may be justified thereby ; that God of his abundant mercy, would vouchsafe to keep you from
all mixture with the dead in spirit, and preserve
you in that state of innocence, from which, at
present, you are under no temptation of departing.   God accepts the unfeigned repentance of
those sinners who have passed away whole years
in guilt, but he is more delighted with the
purity of childhood.   Dedicate, dear children
then, that purity you are possessed of to his service,

...ice, and reflect, that if your purity were but the portion of each individual, sin would less have needed the redeemer's sacrifice, which we have recently commemorated: but God's name be praised, that if he died for our offences, he is risen now, as we have said, to justify us. Be it so, dear children, through the same, our Lord and Saviour Jesus Christ, to whom, &c.

THE HYMN.

JESUS CHRIST is risen to day,	*Hallelujah.*
Rise *you* too, and come away;	*Hallelujah.*
Come away, that you may sing,	*Hallelujah.*
Christ of righteousness the king.	*Hallelujah.*
Come away, that with glad voice,	*Hallelujah.*
Hymning Christ you may rejoice:	*Hallelujah.*
Christ, that suffer'd so much pain	*Hallelujah.*
For our sake, now lives again.	*Hollelujah.*
Come away, that you may sing	*Hallelujah.*
Christ who died to heal our sin,	*Hallelujah.*
Christ, that late resign'd his breath,	*Hallelujah.*
Triumphs now o'er pain and death.	*Hallelujah.*

Come

Come away, that you may raife   *Hallelujah.*
All your voices to his praife: *Hallelujah.*
Chrift, by lying in the grave,   *Hallelujah.*
Died, your fouls from death to fave. *Hallelujah.*

Come away, that you may blefs   *Hallelujah.*
Chrift, your fount of happinefs: *Hallelujah.*
Chrift, whofe flefh the tomb not holds,
                                 Hallelujah.
Rifing, juftifies your fouls.   *Hallelujah.*

SERMON

SERMON XVIII.

ON THE DEARNESS OF CHILDREN
TO GOD.

MARK X. V. 13, 14.

Inscribed to JOSEPH BURCHELL, ESQ. *and his Children,* GEORGIANA, LUCRETIA, LOUI-SA, CATHARINE, *and* HENRY.

And they brought young children to Christ, that he should touch them; and his disciples rebuked those that brought them: but when Jesus saw it, he was much displeased, and said unto them, suffer the little children to come unto me, and forbid them not; for of such is the kingdom of heaven.

YOU, dear little man, who being in the tenderest season of your life, have every need imaginable of a friend to bring you safely up till you arrive at years of reason and reflexion, but as yet, have none, except that father you were born of; for alas! your mother, as

you

you know, departed when that little tongue of
yours could not even lifp her name. you that have
many illneffes infeparable from the people of the
climate you were born in, to endure, you that
at prefent, know not what is learning, and can
fcarcely read a tittle of God's word, you that
muft learn fome bufinefs for fupport, you that
no doubt will wifh to lead a life of virtue in
the world, and are poffeffed of an immortal foul
to fave hereafter,—come dear little man, with
us, and we will introduce you to a friend.

You too, dear little women, who have wants in
common with your brother, but were moulded
of a weaker frame, and have a conftitution not
fo able to encounter hardfhips, you, that having, like your brother, an immortal foul to
fave hereafter, are much opener to temptations,
you that when that beauty God beftowed upon
you, ripened, as we truft it will be by the ftealing
hours of time, fhall fwell into fuch harmonifed
proportions. will be, every way, expofed to the
infidious voice of flattery, to the fuggeftions of
fome youth who will endeavour to exalt you by
his praifes each into a being much above the common daughters of humanity, tho' in the fequel he
reduce you to a creature much beneath them,—
come, dear little maids, with us, and we will
introduce you to a friend.

And

And you too, father of thefe little ones, who while we fpeak are anxious for their pre-fervation and well being in the world, who have received a gift and heritage, as fcripture calls it, from the Lord, but cannot of yourfelf as you are fenfible, protect that heritage from the misfortunes of the world, whofe well be-loved partner poffibly, before the almighty bleffed that marriage fhe had entered into with increafe, might frequently cry out as Rachael, Jacob's wife, did, *give me children or I die;* who faw your Rachael render up the ghoft per-haps in parturition, and who, mourning her un-happy fortune, look on thofe fhe has bequeathed you as the children of your forrow,—come you likewife, much afflicted father, with thefe little pledges of domeftic happinefs (for fuch were they defigned, and fuch by the Almighty's bleffing fhall they be)—oh come and we will in-troduce you likewife to a friend, for can you think him other than a friend to you who will be friendly to your little ones?

That friend is mentioned in this book, where-in whatever is contained, proceeded from his lips. We open it; and what, pray, find you here? Confider it attentively, fond father,

and

and no longer be difcouraged.   Children, read it , and tho' fhe that fhould have reard your infancy is gone, yet ftill have hope.   Firft here, the eighteenth of St. Matthew. *At the fame time, came the difciples unto Jefus, faying, who is the greateft in the kingdom of heaven? and Jefus called a little child, and fet him in the midft of them, and faid. verily I fay unto you, except ye be converted, and become as little children, ye fhall not enter into the kingdom of heaven.*

Whofoever, therefore, fhall humble himfelf as this child, the fame is greateft in the kingdom of heaven; and whofo fhall receive one fuch little child in my name, receiveth me.   But whofo fhall offend one of thefe little ones that believe in me, it were better for him that a mill-ftone were hanged about his neck, and that he were drowned in the depth of the fea.   And once again, a little lower down.   *Take heed that ye defpife not one of thefe little ones; for I fay unto you, that in heaven their angels do always behold the face of my father, which is in heaven.   For the fon of man is come to fave that which was loft.   How think ye? if a man have an hundred fheep, and one of them be gone aftray, doth he not leave the ninety and nine and go into the mountains, and feek that which is*

gone

gone aſtray? And if ſo be that he find it, verily I ſay unto you, he rejoiceth more of that ſheep, than of the ninety and nine which went not aſtray. Even ſo it is not the will of your father which is in heaven that one of thoſe little ones ſhould periſh.

In the next place, here, the tenth of *Mark*, as in the text, *and they brought young children to Chriſt, that he ſhould touch them; and his diſciples rebuked thoſe that brought them: but when Jeſus ſaw it, he was much diſpleaſed; and ſaid unto them, ſuffer the little children to come unto me, and forbid them not; for of ſuch is the kingdom of God: and he took them up in his arms, put his hands upon them, and bleſſed them.*

And is it true, dear little friends, that Jeſus Chriſt, the ſon of God, ſays this? It is. What therefore is the conſequence? that, from his information, it appears you have a friend indeed, a friend whoſe habitation is the heaven of heavens; a friend, who is your God. This is that friend to whom we meant to introduce you, as we ſaid juſt now.

But do you know who Jeſus Chriſt, that ſpoke thus tenderly of little children; do you know we ſay, who Jeſus Chriſt is? Certainly; for you were born of chriſtian parentage, and in a chriſtian land. You are receiving from you father

too,

too, a chriſtian education, and you often read
the teſtament at leaſt, if not the bible likewiſe.
Well, that teſtament contains the life of Jeſus
Chriſt, while he thought proper to reſide among
mankind upon the earth, and, therefore, you
have learned, long ſince, as we can anſwer for
you, who the bleſſed ſon of God is. but, dear
children, God his father has not for theſe many
ages viſited the earth, tho', as you recollect
your catechiſm ſays, in the commandments,
that he viſits the iniquities of fathers on their
children: but this viſiting muſt not be under-
ſtood as when we ſpeak of men or women,
that conſume their time in viſiting each other,
for he dwells in heaven, and his almighty arm
can puniſh wicked people at the greateſt diſ-
tance. therefore, as we ſaid before, he has
not for theſe many ages viſited the earth, nor
did he ever dwell among mankind, as Jeſus
Chriſt did, tho' his bleſſed ſpirit takes up its
abode within the boſom of good men, and,
what is more, in that of children, who are always innocent and lovely.

Liſten therefore, while we tell you what
God is. but, in the mean time, little friends,
be very ſerious, for you cannot be too much ſo,
when his holy name is even mentioned. God,

then,

then, is a being fo immenfely great, that no defcription men are capable of making, can fufficiently fet forth his greatnefs. By his power, you were created, and are kept alive; your eyes, hands, heart, and every faculty you have, were fafhioned by that power, and you belong entirely to him. He made all things, the whole world, and every thing therein. His eye is much more penetrating than the fun at noon. the howling of thofe ftorms, which you have very likely heard without at midnight, being comfortably fheltered and in bed yourfelves, that howling was his voice. His countenance you could not look upon and live, fo powerful is its glory · the full blaze thereof would, in a moment's time, confume you. The whole world, as we have faid, and all things in it are his work; and he is able to deftroy it in an inftant, in as little time as you, if you had fuch a cruel difpofition, could deftroy a helplefs fly, by throwing it into a furnace. By his power, as we have likewife mentioned, you are kept alive, and were he to withdraw his hand, that every moment of the day and night upholds you, then, dear children, you would fall into as many pieces as a brittle bit of glafs, dafhed

violently

violently by a giant's hand, againſt the pave-
ment.

This deſcription puts your little limbs into a
fit of ſhivering: you turn pale, and ſeem to aſk
us if God really is ſuch as we have told you?
Miſerable children as we are! we think we
hear you ſay, where ſhall we hide ourſelves,
next time it thunders, if the tempeſt is God's
voice?   Poor things! be comforted, your ſituation is not ſuch as you imagine, for tho' God
is mighty to do every thing, his mercy is much
greater.   He is in reality your God, but then
he is your father alſo.   Does your earthly father, he now preſent, hate you, little ones? or
can he?   No.   God then, of whoſe abundant
goodneſs it proceeds, and only of his goodneſs,
that this earthly father loves you, God, we ſay,
dear children, neither hates nor can he hate
you· he is love itſelf: he is tremendous, that is
dreadful in his power, but worthy of eternal
praiſe and admiration in his mercy; and this
mercy he diſplays much oftener than his power.   The howling of the tempeſt that affrights
you, when in bed, is in reality his voice; and
ſo too, is the thunder which you often hear at
noon, and which, in your ſimplicity of heart
you are preparing for: but then, the whiſper-
ing

ing breeze that cools you at the hour of fun-fet
is his voice too, like the other. *Who,* fays David, *can abide his frofts?* By his almighty
power the earth is covered with a coat of fnow
in winter; but his mercy foftens the eaft wind,
left it fhould blow too roughly on the innocent
and new caft lamb.

This God, then, whofe benevolence or inclination to do good is fo fuperior to that juftice
which compels him fometimes to afflict us, is
your friend: he loves you; and through Jefus
Chrift, affures young children, that of you, or
as the word may be interpreted, belonging to
you, is his kingdom. You are heirs, by virtue
of your innocence, to everlafting happinefs.
But to affert thus much, and nothing further, is
not faying half enough. You are in fuch a
manner heirs to everlafting happinefs, by virtue
of your innocence, that men and women cannot
be entitled to this happinefs, unlefs before-hand
they become juft like you, for once more, read
over what Chrift Jefus fays to his difciples, in
the 18th of St. Matthew. *Except ye be converted,
and become as little children, ye fhall not enter into
the kingdom of Heaven.* Who could have imagined, little children, God confidered, as he
does, thus kindly of you?

But

But we notice something else; and, as by the above you may, with confidence affert your heirfhip to eternal happinefs, fo likewife by another paffage, you may fee with how much care and caution the Almighty has provided for your happinefs in this world likewife, by fo rigoroufly threatening thofe that fhould offend or do you harm: for once again read this: *Whofo fhall offend one of thefe little ones, that believe in me, it were better for him that a mill-ftone were hanged about his neck, and that he were drowned in the depth of the fea. Take heed, therefore, that ye defpife not one of thefe little ones; for I fay unto you, that in Heaven their angels do always behold the face of my father, which is in Heaven.* So ftrong a hedge it feems, dear children, has your heavenly father placed about your habitation, or, to fpeak more plainly, fuch precaution has he taken, and fuch threats denounced for your fecurity. It were much better for the man that fhall prefume to injure you, that he had never breathed

You, then, to whom thefe five dependants upon providence's favour owe their birth, and who have lately loft that valuable mother they called theirs, but who on her death bed, very likely, in the firm reliance fhe gave proof of,

when

she glanced at your paternal care, to bring them up in virtue, may be said to have expired like Moses in the mount, when he beheld the land of promise at a distance, (for she died, not see-ing, we must own, her children happy in a life of virtue, but assured no doubt, they would be so in future, when led on by your directing hand,) take care that, by a proper cultivation of their ta-lents, you enable them to verify her dying ex-pectations, and that oracle delivered in their favour by the lips of David, when he said: " out of the mouth of babes and sucklings, oh " my God, haft though ordained strength." But how shall they be able to accomplish this pre-diction? By remembering their creator in their tender years, which very likely is the Sa-viour's meaning, when he says,—" One of " these little ones that believe in me." And likewise, in yourself, good friend and brother, let this oracle be verified, for does not God ordain that in the mouth of babes and sucklings, there shall be that strength the psalmist speaks of, when he makes their innocence a model to direct you, since Christ Jesus tells us plainly, that unless we be converted and become like lit-tle children, we shall never have a claim to heaven, which is just as much as saying, be you too a child, and your reward is sure; and since he adds; "whoever shall humble him- "self like a little child, the same is greatest "in the kingdom of heaven, and whoso "shall receive one such little child, in my "name, receiveth me." Adore then, in these great assurances, the providence of God. He gives you children of your body, and those children are your model, by whose innocence, if you resemble it, and do them all the good you can, your soul shall have a place in heaven.

Go therefore, and you too, your earthly fa- ther's lovely little ones, go with him. You possess a friend in heaven; and that friend is he, without whose special leave a sparrow even falls not to the ground: nay further, he that keeps a book, in which the very hairs that grow upon your head are numbered. Go, be happy in this world, and if you part not with your innocence, be sure of happiness hereafter, for can God, who will be finally the awarder of this happiness, dear little ones, de- ny it you? What must not be the tenderness of your creator, when the preacher gazing on you, and particularly so on you, dear Georgi- ana and Lucretia, feels within his bosom such emotions of affection in your favour, as no lan- guage

guage can exprefs? Even now while he is writing, are his fpirits ftrained, if he may fay fo, to the height, and you have taken up his thoughts, till tears roll down upon the paper he bends over. Go, he fays, but gladly would detain you; for like Reuben, coming to the pit where Jofeph had been caft, and finding him not there,—like Reuben, he cries out: *the dear, dear Georgiana and Lucretia are withdrawing; but when two fuch gracious fpirits of affection are (as fpeedily they will be) abfent from me, whither fhall I go?* Till you return, let him employ his thoughts upon you, but employ not you, your thoughts on him, for fhould your gratitude convert itfelf into a love like his,— poor things! you would not, in the weaknefs of your childhood, always longing, as it does, to view the object it has fet its heart on;—no, you would not certainly be able to endure the pain of abfence. May the Almighty pour his blef-fings down upon your head, while you lie fleep-ing in the embraces of each other. Yes, relying on God's promifes, the preacher's hopes inform him of a certainty God *will*; for Jefus fays, *of* you, or as we changed the word before, *belonging* to you, is his father's kingdom.

C 2

Is

Is not this to have a friend? Poor children!
had your heavenly father ordered otherwife, what
then would you have done, for, as at prefent,
you are utterly incapable of any actual fin, you
are incapable of any actual virtue. God accepts
the innocence he gave you, in the place of thofe
good works he looks for at the hand of others
more advanced in years and underftanding. Did
he not, and fhould it pleafe him to put out the
light of being in thofe eyes that fparkle now
with lively pleafure, your afflicted father bend-
ing over you might weep, as David did, while
you were fuffering . but after your deceafe, inftead of being able to confole himfelf, like David, for a little cherub he had loft, by faying:
the poor child, I know is dead, but wherefore
fhould I weep? Can I, by weeping, bring
him back? Myfelf fhall go to him, but he
fhall never come again to me,—your father,
we repeat, would be compelled, in anguifh of
his fpirit, to cry out: oh the unhappy moment! He is gone! His little foul, in a
convulfive pang, made way! He was not of
an age to merit heaven, by any actual virtue!
He departed, though no reprobate, yet ftill no
faint, and I fhall never fee my angel more.

Enable

Fnable us, oh Loid, to praife thy name for all things, but particularly for that gift and heritage of children, thy creating hand beftows upon us. May all parents find them pillars of fupport to reft on in the time of their old age; and may no child, in thofe on whom thou haft beftowed it, want a guide to virtue. May thefe laft be ftruck with awe, in contemplating thy ftrict juftice, and abftain from all iniquity, left thou fhouldft vifit them in their defcendants: fo, when full of years, the parent of his family repofes everlaftingly in Abraham's bofom, fhall thofe children he taught righteoufnefs, invoke upon themfelves the certain mercies he was crowned with, and inherit the fure bleffings of a long and happy life, which by thy law is pro-mifed, in the land we live in. Hear us for the fake of Jefus Chrift, &c.

THE HYMN.

TO celebrate thy name, oh Lord,
   Our voices let us raife :
Thou wilt not turn away thine ear,
   When children fing thy praife.

        Thy

Thy providence our fafeguard was,
    While in the womb we grew ;
And, when upon the breaft we hung,
    From ills it fav'd us too.

Safe to this hour, thy guardian care
    Has led us by the hand,
Thro' ficknefs, and thro' other ills,
    A formidable band.

Of thy abundant love it comes,
    That thofe who gave us breath,
Would to promote our benefit,
    Expofe themfelves to death.

If from this caufe then fuch their love,
    Dear God how can it be,
But that, as Jefus Chrift has faid,
    We muft be dear to thee ?

Then for thy love, thus prompting theirs,
    Our thanks, Lord, let us fhow ;
Though we can never as we ought,
    Repay them half we owe.

                                    But

But if our gratitude we prove
    With all our heart and might,
Poor though the gift! yet shall it be
    Well pleasing in thy sight.

f

SERMON XIX.

ON DRESS.

MATTHEW v v. 28.

Why take ye thought for raiment?

WE begin this exhortation, little friends
and hearers, by obferving, that provided we can point you out the vanity of
every boaft annexed to drefs, we fhall go very
far in our endeavours to prevent you now,
while you are young, from giving way to any
paffionate defires of being, as it were, diftin-
guifhable among other children by that outward
finery, which, to the fhame of human nature
be it faid, too many of the prefent age affeft,
for can there be a greater fhame to human nature, than that men, yes men, we fay, as well
as women, in their rage for drefs, in their defire,
their anxious wifh to vie with one another in
the beauty, elegance and fafhion of the garments they put on, fhould yield themfelves in
fuch a manner to that rage, to that defire, that

anxious

anxious wifh, as in a very little fpace of time
to ruin their affairs, by that expence fine cloaths,
require? One would fuppofe, however, that at
laft, when they behold the ruinous effects
attendant on their pride, and the deficience of
that money which has all been lavifhed on the
article of drefs, while other preffing wants are
unfupplied, the wifh of being thus diftinguifhed in the company they cannot keep from
mingling with, would ceafe:—but no,—the
pride of being fine, continues even then, though
while they gratify it, they are forced to argue
with themfelves as follows ·—" We will fuffer
" filently—we will contrive to go without much
" greater comforts and conveniences—we will
" keep back the wages of domeftic fervants—
" we will totally neglect the obligations on us
" to give alms—we will not cherifh a paternal
" or maternal difpofition towards our children,
" which is moft effectually fhown by giving them
" a proper education—in a word, we will confent
" to pinch our bellies, that our backs may be pro-
" vided for, we will do this, and more, if only we
" may make a figure in the world. We will digeft
" what others might conceive the anguifh of a ftate
" of poverty," (the anguifh of a ftate of poverty
your preacher, by the bye, remarks, when men
have brought it on themfelves,) " and not com-

C 5   " plain,

" plain, provided we may be more gaudily
" dreffed out than others." Can we poffibly
conceive fo monftrous a caprice, to call it by
the fofteft appellation language can apply?

From this caprice, God giant, dear little
friends and hearers, you may be exempt, and
that you may be fo, attentively confider what
we have to offer, while we fhow you, as was
mentioned at the opening of this difcourfe, the
vanity of every boaft annexed to drefs, by
pointing out that nothing in the world can be
more changeable than what is looked upon as
elegance therein. No, nothing in the world
can be more changeable than the affair of drefs,
in which what poffibly might be confidered
beautiful twelve months ago, will now be laugh-
ed at, and in twelve months time, perhaps,
admired again This change is not the character of arts and virtue, which are therefore
worth affecting, and fit objects to excite our
zeal; a truth that cannot be advanced refpecting drefs. But we proceed with what we
meant to lay before you for confideration, with
regard to finery in drefs: to prove it fuch, we
have a very certain method, and a method
which the youngeft of you will not be perplexed
to comprehend. Let any picture be produced,

exhibiting

exhibiting what well-dreſſed children were ſome years ago, that is, exhibiting what ſort of clothes they wore. Why, you would laugh at their groteſque appearance. What ſtrange figures ! you would cry, and poſſibly burſt out into a fit of laughter at the ſight. So too, no doubt, if you could ſee a picture repreſenting well-dreſſed children, ſuch as they will be in point of dreſs as many years hereafter, you would laugh as much as in the former caſe, comparing what they would be then, with what they are at preſent, for in every thing, and more particularly dreſs, wherein the vanity of mortals has ſo large a field to range in, faſhion is perpetually ſhifting, nothing being conſtantly the ſame but arts and virtue.

After this, dear little friends, will you go on deſiring to be finely dreſſed, when, for a year together no one can define what in reality is the diſtinguiſhing criterion mark or feature of fine dreſs ? But we miſtake ourſelves, for in the eſtimation of a reaſonable creature, to be finely dreſſed is to exhibit, in the faireſt point of view, all that delightful ſymmetry, or all thoſe beauties of proportion nature has beſtowed upon the human form and figure, juſt as to dance well, is to deport one's ſelf with all that

C 6

grace

grace and eafe of which we are fufceptible by nature, he that fhould go farther, being nothing but a tumbler, pofture-mafter, or the like, who may do very well to entertain a noify theatre, but not give pleafure to, or gain applaufe from, company in private life.

Hence, therefore, may we draw the following queftion, namely: If the prefent mode of drefs for children beft fets off their gracious form and figure, (*beft*, for it confifts with reafon to fuppofe that, granting parents, anxious as they are to place their children's native beauties in the faireft point of view, were fenfible of any other drefs more fuited to that end, they would adopt it) if, we fay, the prefent mode of drefs for children beft fets off their gracious form and figure, for fure gracious may we call it, being, as it is, the great Creator's work, and captivating, as it does, all eyes, and if the grand criterion or diftinction of that drefs be, what it is at prefent, abfolute fimplicity—*no article too much about it*, why, when by the progrefs of perhaps a dozen years, when the fimplicity of childhood is in fome degree worn off, do individuals have recourfe for ornament to that complexity of drefs, to *that too much about it,* which the prefent generation of adults,

or

or grown up perfons, wear? Is it becaufe the
human countenance is changed in its proportions? No, dear little friends, the worft that
can be faid of womanly or manly grace or
beauty, is as follows: That the Almighty's
work, in fuch as have attained to their maturity, is only lefs enchanting, in proportion as
the individual has gone forward from the years
of childhood. It is not, in any fenfe of the
expreffion, unattractive, it is only lefs attrac-
tive. Carefully confider this, and you will fee
that the fimplicity of drefs in children fhould
not, as it does, give place to fo much fuper-
fluity, to any whim that fafhion may induce
the foolifh, or at leaft the thoughtlefs, or to
mend the expreffion, thofe who take no thought
except for raiment to make ufe of, when their
children are much nearer men and women.

Would to God we could prevail upon your
candid minds *to take no thought for raiment*, as
the text expreffes it, or to adopt at leaft an
abfolute indifference, not to fay an utter fcorn
of every unbecoming ornament in drefs, it
would, when you grow men or women, fave
you from a world of trouble and anxiety. Of
every *unbecoming* ornament of drefs, we fay,
there being ornaments of drefs that may with
safety

fafety be adopted, for St. Paul himſelf, in one of his Epiſtles, ſays, *I will that women adorn themſelves,* and ſo forth. Neither are we to ſuppoſe that even gold and ſilver are at all times totally forbidden. The great rule is this—that all the ornaments of dreſs we may adopt, be ſuited to our rank and ſituation, and indeed it ſeems, that all the extravagance of dreſs ſo much in vogue among us, is adopted by the multitude, who do not think what ornaments will really become them. Surely we are au-thoriſed to ſay thus much, for if we were not thoughtleſs, would the ſervant maid ſet off her perſon juſt as if ſhe were the miſtreſs? or the man who lives by a profeſſion, imitate the dreſs of noblemen, and ſo forth? But we cut the matter very ſhort, by urging, that in every walk of life, men do wrong things for want of due reflection, and of courſe, in dreſs. It is not likely that the man or woman who may think it fitting to debate what dreſs will ſuit particular occaſions, ranks, or ſituations in the world, will fix on an improper or indecent per-ſonal adornment. All the fault is, that we do not think in any manner. We experience not the conſolation in our errors to alledge that we have previouſly thought wrong. Our judgment

cannot

cannot err as often as our will is led aftray. Did we yield up our will to be directed by our judgment, we fhould act with more propriety than we do act in common. If we would but once refolve upon confulting our ideas of propriety in drefs, we fhould difcern the truth of this remark, *videlicet*: that the intrinfi. ornament we ought to have recourfe to, and particularly what the female world fhould be obfervant of, is the neglect of ornament.

" Behold," fays Jefus Chrift, alluding to the almoft favage garb of his fore-runner in the wildernefs, the camel's hair and leathern girdle of St. John the Baptift, " they who wear " foft raiment live in courts ," or, as he fays, " kings' houfes." But fince then, the times are marvelloufly altered, fo that now the rougher fex are no lefs ftudious to adorn their perfons, than the gentler part of the creation, whofe foft character may plead fome right to perfonal adornment. But to them, that is the men, we wifh not in this exhortation to addrefs ourfelf ; for if the fhame of their indulging in a practice fo effeminate cannot contribute to affect them, their unmanly conduct is far gone indeed. but we addrefs ourfelf to thofe who plead their right, as being females, to purfue a female practice ;

and

and to them, we fay, that in no point of view
can their attachment to that tyrant fafhion, in
the article of drefs, be any way excufed, for
women, and particularly thofe who are not yet
united in the bands of wedlock with a hufband,
may alledge they have a right or title to affect a
brilliancy, becaufe they are convinced it fets off
beauty, and becaufe a hufband may reward
them, but we anfwer, that a hufband, fuch as
is acknowledged worth poffeffing, can be gained by no demeanour other than what modefly
fuggefts. Their vanity indeed may be amufed
by fraud and fallacy, and lovers fuch as they are
called, by *fictious* paffions and vain proteftati-
ons may endeavour to infpire their tender bofoms with a real paffion, fuch as cannot be, by
them at leaft, returned, in kind. Such lovers
every day are to be met with; but are thefe
the characters that reafonable women fhould
affect for hufbands? reafonable women, that
in marrying conftantly look out for happinefs?
Befides, while women are defirous thus to
pleafe beholders by their outward drefs, they
muft eternally be in the fafhion, and already we
have fhown you the inconftancy of fafhion,
that is fcarcely ever the fame thing a month together.   And if fo, how monftrous is not
that

that degree of fervitude when you reflect,—and you, young people, that are prefent be attentive to the obfervation,—that this thing called fafhion, will be liable to twenty changes in the world, before you can expect to reap the benefit you aim at, by thus always being in the fafhion.

This, dear little friends we are aware before you tell us fo, has been a theme, that in difcuffing it by no means can have given you much pleafure. It includes however an inftruction that, provided you attend thereto, will at a future period, tho' not now, be beneficial to you. Jefus Chrift has, in his fermon on the mount, advanced a truth fufficient one would think to mortify the pride of thofe who turn their ftudy to the embellifhments of drefs, by faying; and what now we are about to mention, is the paffage out of which our text has been felected, namely: *why take ye thought for raiment? confider the lillies of the field, how they grow: they toil not; neither do they fpin. And tey, I fay unto you, that even Solomon in all his glory, was not arrayed like one of thefe.* From this quotation it appears, dear children, that the monarch of the eaft, in all his regal greatnefs, in the purple worn by kings, and with

the

the diadem upon his head, was not fo glorious
as a fimple lilly of the field ; and for this fpecial
reafon, fince the glory of king Solomon, that
glory Jefus Chrift referred to, with his purple
robe and diadem, was fabricated by men's
hands, whereas the fplendor of the lilly is
God's work.—Ye lillies of the field, as we may
call you, that particularly in this exhortation we
have preached to, you, in every region of whofe
countenance is to be feen the fnowy fplendour
of the lilly, mingled with the vernal blufhes of
the rofe, may God preferve you in that happy
innocence of heart, of which whoever is poffefs-
ed, knows neither that pale caft of thought, nor
thofe diftempered burnings of confufion, which
clofe guilt or affectation frequently diffufes over
the whole cheek. Since beauty is the gift of heaven, cherifh that beauteous form which every one
of you may have received, and think it the adornment of a temple framed for the Almighty's holy
fpirit to inhabit. Let that boaft, fweet hearers, be
your only pride. All other ornaments ferve only
to keep vanity alive ; and fhe that would admi-
nifter to fuch a paffion, muft in reafon pafs for
vanity herfelf   And you, that with lefs right
to a difplay of drefs, may have as ftrong an inclination, tho' not half the opportunity, confi-
                                                    der

der that the major part of what you wear is but the fpoil of fome poor fheep, or what the filk worm has procured you. Strong diffuafives both, one would fuppofe, againft the pride of coftly clothes. May God improve the feed that has been fown at prefent in your hearts, thro' Jefus Chrift our Lord, &c.

THE HYMN.

WHENE'ER along the road I walk,
    Or thro' the crowded ftreet,
How many little ones forlorn
    And deftitute, I meet!

With rags, that fcarce their body hide,
    And naked feet they go,
Poor wretched things! through wet and dirt,
    And hail and rain and fnow.

While I, before a good fire-fide,
    May warm myfelf all day:
And when I walk abroad, have clothes
    To keep the cold away.

Yet

Yet let me not be proud or vain
    Of ought I have to wear,
Nor on poor children look with scorn
    Whose limbs are almost bare.

But now and then, while inly griev'd
    I pity their distress,
Get leave with some cast clothes of mine,
    To hide their nakedness.

SERMON

SERMON XX.

ON CARD PLAYING.

PROVERBS XVI. V. 33.

The lot is caft into the lap, but the whole dif-posing thereof is of the Lord.

THE book of Proverbs, little children, was compofed or written by king Solomon, the wifeft man that ever lived. A proverb is a faying full of meaning, and expreffed in fuch a manner as to ftrike the mind. In proverbs, all the learning of the common fort of people in the feveral regions of the world, was formerly contained, when they had not the benefit of books to teach them, and in many regions of the world, this want of books, occafioned by the want of printing, ftill fubfifts. The book of proverbs in the Bible, has one great advantage over every other fet of proverbs, which is this, that while, like other proverbs, they contain a deal of information,

and

and a deal of learning, they were written under the immediate infpiration of God's holy
fpirit, in the heart of Solomon, for Solomon
we need not tell you, was a prophet, that is,
one inftructed by the Almighty to fortel fuch
things as fhould in future come to pafs. It
follows then from this, that while the truth of
other proverbs may be called in queftion, thefe
are truth itfelf, and one of thefe indubitable
truths is *that* which we have chofen for our
text. *The lot is caft into the lap, but the whole
difpofing thereof is of the Lord.*

The circumftance of cafting lots feems nothing more than what even you have frequently
recourfe to, when you hold out feveral lengths
of paper in your hand, and fee which of your
company fhall draw the longeft; when you
guefs as the expreffion is at *odd* or *even*, and
the like. It is determining fome point in fuch
away as fhall not in the leaft depend upon
yourfelves. Now, nothing more is meant by
what the prophet tells us, when he fays, the
lot is caft into the lap.

One obfervation we muft notwithftanding
make. You do not think that when you
feek amufement from the act of drawing forth
the longeft bit of paper out of feveral lengths,

when you guefs at *odd* or *even*, or the like, you do not think, we fay, you are engaged in any ferious bufinefs, but of old, this mode of drawing lots was inftituted to decide the greateft matters, and to fettle peace among the powerful, who would otherwife have been fierce foes: thus in the eighteenth chapter of the Proverbs. *The lot caufeth contention to ceafe, and parteth between the mighty*. and to give another from the fecond chapter of the Acts, this method of the lot, accompanied by prayer, was had recourfe to for the purpofe of determining, of two difciples, which was to be numbered with the reft, and fill the place of Judas who had hanged himfelf, for felling or betraying Jefus. *They appointed two*, fays the Evangelift, *Jofeph called Barnabas, who was furnamed Juftus, and Matthias, and they prayed, and faid, thou Lord which knoweft the hearts of all men, fhow whether of thefe two thou haft chofen, that he may take part of this miniftry and apoftlefhip, from which Judas, by tranfgreffion, fell, that he might go to his own place. And they gave forth their lots, and the lot fell upon Matthias, and he was numbered with the eleven apoftles.*

All that has been hitherto advanced is nothing but by way of preface to this exhortation, which the

text is meant to introduce : that preface being
finifhed, we proceed, dear children, to our
fubject, and obferve, that if this method of
determining events by circumftances independent of our will or pleafure were not made fub-
fervient to bad purpofes, it might be innocently had recourfe to, in the prefent days, by thofe
who fit together at a table, and apparently depend on the decifion of what men call *chance*
for THOUSANDS, in a fpace of time no longer
frequertly, than what is neceffary to pronounce
the word.

We fay apparently, for the reverfe is really
the cafe: fince men, remarkable for nothing
but their fubtilty, avail themfelves of this fuppofed equality between all thofe who are engaged together, and by virtue of a number of
contrivances, on which, becaufe we are not
converfant in the fociety of fuch adventurers,
we are not competent to fay a fyllable, but only know that fuch contrivances do really exift,
by virtue of a number of contrivances, we fay,
find means to cheat their thoughtlefs neighbour
or companion.

Now, among too many engines thus made
ufe of in the way of chance, as we have juft
now called it, every one productive of bad
con-

confequences, and the ruin of whole families ; but this which we are going to defcribe, particularly ftigmatized by law, are certain oblong pafte-boards, fpotted black and red, to which thofe, ufing them moft innocently, have recourfe as regularly as the evening comes, that they may either wile away the tedious time, or fhun temptations to afperfe or vilify the fame and credit of their neighbours, while the reft employ them to replenifh, that is, fill their purfes with the money gleaned from friends ; in which avidity too many care not in what ftate of penury they leave thofe friends, provided only they can fave their own exceptionable characters, by having it to boaft that thofe with whom they played, were fairly foiled or beaten in the conteft, though of thefe, no few demur not by felonious fchemes to plunder fuch as ftruggle with them for the maftery in thofe difputes, wherein fome fay chance fettles every thing. Hence therefore, very commonly as we have faid already, penury enfues to thofe rafh dupes that have engaged therein ; and, horrible idea, not unfrequently defpair and death !

Ill fated ***! unhappy youth! if you could leave that grave, to which, in an untimely

moment, your own hand, which the unhappy lofs
of every thing you were poffeffed of, aimed
with defperation, plunged you! were this poffible, we fay, you would ftand forth a melancholy proof of what we have afferted. Early
were you trained, beneath the roof of your
unthoughtful parents, to this fatal way of diffipating precious time. They had no manner
of employment, they had run their round of
pleafure in the fafhionable world, and had fo
often fled for refuge from the pain of thought,
to fuch amufements as are current in the age,
that thofe amufements were [themfelves fa-
tiguing. Every evening therefore fat they down,
amid the circle of their friends, all eager as it
were for plunder from each other, and with
hands that fhook at once thro' avarice and age,
dealt the deftructive implements of their irrational diverfion round the board. You too, unhappy "**, were with them, even in the tendereft feafon of your youth, when to your choice
it muft have been a matter of indifference,
what amufement you reforted to. Alas! they
fhould have thought, not only then, but even
afterward, before the habit was quite rooted
in you, that like them, you had not run the
gant-loop, as fome people fay, of pleafure,

and

and might eafily have reaped enjoyment from
ten thoufand objects both in art and nature,
rather than this curfed way of wafting time.
But no · your ruin was determined on ; and to
increafe the mifery, poor youth ! your parents
were to feal the fentence that condemned you.
Under their inhofpitable roof, not fo indeed to
others, who attended every morning for the
copious overflowing of the former day's abundance on their table, but feverely fo to you,
fince you received no other portion than that
modifh education which alas, while others
hold their children out an education meant at
leaft to get them bread, they, horrid to relate!
were careful to provi'e you, fcarcely dream-
ing it would be a ftone to grind your fubftance
into atoms, and much lefs imagining it bore
the likenefs of a ferpent, fuch as might in future hifs and fting your very being,—under
their inhofpitable roof, we fay, you were too
carefully and cruelly brought up, a victim dedicated to deftruction, and adorned before the
knife was to perform its office. You faw both
your parents pay their debt to nature, and foon
after quitted England, to enjoy the pleafures
of a foreign country, with the opportunities of
gleaning profit or improvement in a fchool,

D 2   which,

which, from its confequences, proved to you
fo fatal. You fet out, firft taking leave of
one, with whom, on your return, you were
to join your fortunes by a union the moft facred and endearing. You were feparated foon
by many leagues of land and water from your
native country, but took with you the accom-
plifhment, the art or fcience you had previoufly
acquired in that academy, where your mifguid-
ed parents had prefided, while you made fo fa-
tisfactory a progrefs. You renewed your ftu-
dies at a famous place, where fafhion dictates
that refort of company, which every year
crouds to it, from a notion that its waters will
repair a broken conftitution : this indeed is the
pretext ; but diffipation beckons from her throne,
and in the feveral countries round about it,
multitudes obey the fummons, and are mingled with a croud of thofe, who being always on
the watch to lure the unwary, do more mifchief
than the waters of the place, with all their
boafted qualities, at any time do good. You
entered into this fociety of harpies: in one
night, by their feloniou- practices, they ftripped
you of a patrimony, and in fome fort left you
no lefs naked than the new born child. and
would to God! we could but add to this def-

cription,

cription, no lefs harmlefs. You were now
reduced to nothing. All your land in England
irretrievably was pledged to your undoers; and
where then were you, condemned as you yourfelf exprefled it, to endure an odious being, you
had not fo much belonging to you, as would
be enough to purchafe you the fad pofleflion of
a grave; for, on that melancholy object, were
your thoughts now fettled. You were tired of
life, and there were things, called piftols, for
the wretched to refort to. Read, dear children,
read the letter this unhappy prodigal compofed
before his putting to both temples two of thofe
deftructive weapons juft now fpoken of, and
which he left behid him for the information
of the living. Read it, and by fuitable reflections, fpare your preacher the afflicting tafk of
profecuting this unhappy ftory.

" I have paid my debt to fortune, and to
" nature. I have left two louis d'ors (*about*
" *two guineas)* in the public alms-box, for
" the benefit of thofe who are not to be charg-
" ed with having made themfelves as indigent
" as I am. Thefe two louis d'ors are all I
" am poffeffed of, after rifing mafter of fome
" thoufands, in the morning, for the laft laft
" time before I fall, as foon I fhall, for ever.

D 3 " You

" You, that read this letter, pity me. My
" debts, as they are called, of *honor*, are al-
" ready paid, for had I been unwilling to dif-
" charge them, thofe who were the winners,
" would have forced me to preferve my charac-
" ter. There is an amiable and virtuous lady.
" —She—Ah God"——

And here he ended. the reproaches of his
foul, and perturbation of his thoughts, would not
permit him to conclude this letter. It is more,
alas! than what will ferve us as a warning to
deter you from a fpecies of amufement that
brought down fo dreadful a cataftrophe on this
unhappy youth ; for how, dear children, know
you but that granting you give way, as he did,
to a cuftom fo feducing, you will afterward incur his wretched exit. Should you afk us
whether we fuppofe it likely you fhould meet
with fuch a melancholy fortune, if you have recourfe to fuch a fpecies of amufement as he
pitched on,—rather than make anfwer to that
queftion, we will afk *you* one, which may comprize within it the whole force of that reply
you need· and that is, whether we fhould
think it likely you will meet with fuch a melancholy fortune, if you do *not* have recourfe to
fuch a fpecies of amufement as he pitched on ?

Hence,

Hence, without deciding on the confequence that may or may not follow your indulging in a habit that has proved deftructive to fuch multitudes already, we may put the following cafe, as lawyers call it —Let there, in the firft place, be a fafhionable way of paffing time among us, which *may* end in difmal confequences, but can never have a happy iffue. let there, in the next place, be another way of paffing time among us, which can never end in difmal confequences, but may have a happy iffue,—which of thefe two ways of paffing time, although one may indeed be fafhionable, would you chufe, dear children?

The preceding obfervations we have put together for your benefit, though after all, the following admonition, which will likewife be of ufe in many other cafes, may fuit here. We give it with the greater pleafure, as by doing fo, we fhun the imputation of all fingularity in faying, that the ufe of cards, as an amufement, is an anti-chriftian way of paffing time. The admonition is as follows. when you happen to have nothing better you can do, then go to cards, and you will not be anfwerable for a fin; at leaft, dear children, greater than of

D 4 doing

doing what you had it in your contemplation otherwife to do. With this we finifh, firft of all befeeching God, that not alone in greater mat- ters, but in this too of your recreation, he will gracioufly inform your underftanding   Father of the world, whofe power at the beginning of the world or time, compleated that great plan thy wifdom had conceived beforehand, it was thou that gaveft thefe little ones affembled in thy prefence that activity of limb they run with; that endoweft them with that cheerfulnefs of feature which fuffufes their whole countenance, when any thing delights them, and that makeft their playfulnefs of action fo endearing to all thofe who gaze upon them.   We are fenfible that nothing thou beftoweft, has been conferred except to anfwer fome great purpofe.   Conde- cend then to conduct this little congregation met together in thy name, in fuch a manner that if ferious occupations or exhilarating paf- times take up their attention, every thing they are engaged in may contribute to thy glory. Does not David call on dragons, all deeps, to celebrate thy praifes? Why then may not thefe before thee, in their fports and recreati- ons, magnify thy holy name.   They may.
Vouch-

Vouchfafe then, that in every action of their lives, they may evince their innocence, through Jefus Chrift, &c.

THE HYMN,

OH Lord, fince in thy word we're taught,
That to thy-glory fhould be wrought
    Whatever I may do,
Vouchfafe that ee'n fuch fport and play
As in thy fight feems good, I may
    Be careful to purfue.

My fport and play thou wilt not fure
Confider finful or impure,
    Oh no, for thou on earth
Beholdft from thy celeftial height,
The creatures fporting in thy fight,
    Pleas'd with the general mirth.

D 5   Then

Then not from fport and play, let me
Faftidious turn, left thou fhouldft fee,
   And feeing take offence:
But through my mind, thy grace diffufe,
Such fport and play that I may chufe
   As fuits my innocence.

SERMON

SERMON XXI,

ON BECOMING CONVERSATION.

JAMES III. V. 13.

Who is a wife man, and endued with knowledge amongft you? Let him fhew out of a good converfation his works.

WHAT the apoftle means by that *wife* man he fpeaks of, is a *virtuous* man, which alteration being made, the text, we apprehend, is to the following purport. He, among you, that would gain a character of virtue, let him pay attention to his converfation. Now the inftrument of converfation, we need hardly tell you, little children, is the tongue: it follows then, that he who would obtain a character of virtue, in the firft place fhould take care to regulate the office of his tongue.

What reafon can be given, that this regulation of the tongue is fo particularly neceffary to acquire the character of virtue? Probably fince, to diftinguifh us from brutes, we had the

D 6   faculty

faculty of fpeech beftowed upon us, and fince he who fain would lead a virtuous life, does but defire to lead a life, as Solomon defines it, different from brute beafts that perifh ; probably on this account, the regulation of that organ neceffary in the act of fpeaking is expedient: for we know that fome men's converfation is of fuch a kind, that notwithftanding they, as well as all their fellow creatures, have received a tongue, to render them more excellent than brutes, they ufe it after fuch a manner that it finks them much below thofe brutes.

Accordingly, the fame apoftle, who fupplies our text, has, in a verfe or two before it, reckoned up fome few among the many wicked purpofes, whereto the tongue is frequently applied, which wicked purpofes, that he may put their vilenefs in much ftronger colours, he contrafts with thofe good purpofes that are directly oppofite thereto. Thus, if you look four verfes higher than the text, or at the ninth, he fays, as you will find: *therewith*, before-hand having fpoken of the tongue, *blefs we God, even the father; and therewith, curfe we men who are made after the fimilitude of God: out of the fame mouth proceed blessing and curfes.*

After

After which he adds : *my brethren, these things ought not to be.* These words, we must confess, convey no very grievous censure; but the practice they refer to, must be certainly acknowledged very grievous. It appears then that the apostle, having told us how extremely wicked men can be, so wicked as to curse God's likeness with that tongue which others use to bless their maker, is so shocked at the exceeding sinfulness of such a practice, that he cannot find fit words to stigmatize it, just as if ourselves should say, in reference to any sin we had been talking of, *it is a crime so shocking that we know not what to call it.*

In reality, no duty is so often taken notice of in scripture as that government the tongue should be brought under; for not only does the apostle James advert to this important duty, but the major part of what are called the sacred writers: thus, the Psalmist: *Keep thy tongue from evil*; and again, *I said I will take heed to my ways, that I offend not with my tongue:* and Solomon, among his proverbs; *Death and life are in the power of the tongue; and whoso keepeth his mouth and his tongue, keepeth his soul from trouble:* and the author of our text; *If any man among you seem to be religious, and bridleth*

not

not his tongue, but deceiveth his own heart, that man's religion is vain. To which we are to add a verse or two extracted from the chapter out of which our text is taken, that relate particularly to this duty, and contain expressions which we would not dare assert upon our own authority, but which it is expedient, little friends, you should be made acquainted with, that you may have a just idea of the obligation you are under to restrain, betimes, the freedom of your tongue. He introduces his remarks and observations on this duty, by informing those he writes to, that *if any man offend not in word, the same is a perfect man, and able also to bridle the whole body. Behold,* he then continues, *we put bits in horses' mouths that they may obey us, and we turn about their whole body. behold also the ships, which, though they be so great, and are driven of fierce winds, yet are they turned about with a small helm, whithersoever the governor listeth Even so, the tongue is a little member and boasteth great things Behold, how great a matter a little fire kindleth ! and the tongue is a fire ! a world of iniquity ! so is the tongue among our members, that it defileth the whole body, and setteth on fire the course of nature, and is set on fire of Hell; for every kind of beasts and of birds, and of serpents,*

ferpents, and things in the fea is tamed, and hath
been tamed of mankind: but the tongue can no mare
tame: it is an unruly evil, full of deadly poifon.

Thus far the apoftle. If the cafe then really be
fo, why was the gift of fpeech beftowed on
human beings, and what reafon could the
pfalmift have to fay, that for the goodnefs God
had fhewn him, he would praife his mercy
with the beft, for fo he calls it, *the beft member*
he poffeffed? If, as the apoftle fays, our tongue
doth fet on fire the courfe of nature, and is fet
on fire of Hell, to what good office can it be
applied? no lefs, dear children, than the offices
of praying to, and praifing the Almighty.
Thefe, in fact, we muft acknowledge, are employments worthy of it: thofe hard cenfures
which the apoftle, as already we have faid, has
paffed upon it, are not, we confefs, ill founded:
but the tongue is fuch, as with the greateft
truth he has defcribed it, not from any want
of goodnefs (be it fpoke with reverence) in the
great creator, but from our corrupt and wicked
difpofitions, that we turn the greateft bleffings
into curfes: witnefs riches, in refpect of which
the Saviour has informed us, that a camel
fhall, with much more eafe, pafs through a
needle's eye, than any rich man enter into
Heaven:

Heaven: though David, fpeaking from the influence of God's fpirit, has beftowed the following panegyric on them, or on thofe who ufe their riches in the exercife of charitable actions: *Bleffed is the man that fhall relieve the poor and needy; God fhall fend him fuccour in the time of trouble:* but the difference between thefe two opinions may be eafily accounted for ; as David had in view the worthy ufe of riches, and Chrift Jefus their abufe. The fame is to be faid refpecting any other things called *good* in life, which was intended to be fo , but which mankind, by yielding to the wicked one's fuggeftions, have contaminated or debafed. We have already faid, in favour of the tongue, that we might prove it the beft member a religious man can have, that it was firft of all beftowed upon us to difcharge the offices of prayer and praife. Thefe are employments, on the part of men, moft pleafing to the great creator: and let no one look upon that inftrument, which the Almighty has beftowed upon us for fo good a purpofe, as he would do on a gift defigned for our deftruction.

But what follows from this ufe to which the tongue may be applied? much follows from

it,

it, children. Hear then with attention, fince
the intimation may become of fignal benefit to
you who are in fuch a ftage of life, that you
may make a virtuous conduct not fo meritorious
as habitual to your nature ; namely, that provided you have any notion of religion, gratitude
to God, or decency among mankind, you will
at no time fo profane that tongue, which was
beftowed upon you for the purpofes of praying
to, and praifing God, as to employ it in the
way of execration, as fome do, that (horrid to
relate!) have curfed not only men, made after
the fimilitude, as James informs us, of their
maker, but their very maker likewife. Well
then did the wife of Job, when fhe advifed her
hufband to fo horrible a crime as that of
curfing God, add afterwards, " and die." *Curfe
God,* faid fhe, *and die* : but in what words did
the unhappy Job make anfwer ? The diftrefs
he fuffered, the intolerably painful boils and
ulcers fpread all over him, and the afflicting
hand of poverty, that, after he had been fo
wealthy, wrung his foul, together with the
lofs of all his children, that he thought had
perifhed—all thefe miferies together, did not
caufe him to forget that from the liberality
of God he had received that cheerfulnefs of

heart

heart which then had quitted him , that foundnefs which was utterly corrupted with fo many
fores , that wealth, to which fuch want of all
things had fucceeded , and that houfe full lately of beloved children, but in which all fud-
denly was defolate, at leaft as he imagined.
He had not forgot, we fay, that all thefe bleffings had proceeded from the liberality of God,
who might with juftice take them from him ;
and that tongue which, when the news was
brought him of his flocks, his fervants, and his
children, all at once thus taken from him,
could not only fo religioufly abftain from every
accent of complaint, but after he had fallen
proftrate on the ground, confefs as follows:
*Naked came I firft of all into the world, and naked
I fhall leave it too.   It was the Lord that gave;
and it is now the Lord that takes away   Be therefore
his almighty name for ever bleffed of me*   Yes, that
tongue which proved its much afflicted but refigned poffeffor, to be really a wife or virtuous
man, endued with knowledge, and one, likewife,
who would fhew his works by what the text,
as you remember, calls good converfation ,—
we repeat, that tongue, dear children, which
could give fuch proof of refignation to God's
will, was fatisfied with anfwering, when his
                                             wife

wife advifed him to curfe God, and die when he had curfed him, that *fhe fpoke as one among the foolifh women fpeaks for fhall mankind receive*, that is, be always praying to receive *good things from God, and fhall they not receive,* that is, fubmit with thankfulnefs when they are vifited with *evil things?* Thus far the pious Job, whofe wife's pernicious, not to call it wicked, counfel, *tingles ftill,* as was God's word to Samuel, when he meant to execute the purpofe of his wrath, *in both my ears.* Curfe God! the power that loves us! and while tyrants here on earth are boafting of the mifchief they can do their fellow creatures, fhews his goodnefs daily! If, indeed, the wickednefs of nature can prevail upon my heart fo far as to curfe God, let me, if poffible, die after, and be utterly extinct, not render up the ghoft with any notion of the poffibility there is, that in another world I fhall furvive where men muft either live in the eternal funfhine of his love, or groan beneath the frown of his eternal wrath. I cannot live in this world, if God's love does not fupport me: how then fhall I live hereafter in the condemnation of God's hatred, and endure the everlafting weight of his uplifted arm?

By

By this time we have faid enough, dear little ones, to put you on your guard againſt the crime of giving up that tongue to profanation, which was made for prayer and praiſe. And yet we ſtop not here, for weighing well the dignity of theſe two offices, and how exceedingly they pleaſe God's ear, you will not vilify your tongue with falſity, or (if ſuch uſe as we are going now to mention can be poſſibly avoided) even trifling converſation: for this trifling converſation is condemnable, if you compare it with that prayer and praiſe which in themſelves are ſo exalted, and may occupy your tongues. It was not, therefore a hard ſaying of Chriſt Jeſus, as the twelve remarked, reſpecting what he had been telling them, though on another buſineſs, that his father would bring every idle word, as he expreſſed it, into judgment, which mankind ſhould ſpeak, for what occaſion is there, little friends, for idle converſation, when that love we ought to have for God may furniſh every moment ſuch delightful topics of diſcourſe, and ſuch as is ſo far from being idle, that God's ſpirit is delighted with it? And, indeed, how can it poſſibly be otherwiſe? How can the love of God frame any topics of diſcourſe, but what his holy ſpirit muſt be pleaſed with? We,

for

for our part, from the love of many we could
name among you, can derive such arguments
as marvelously help us forward on this subject.
You, dear *Ann* and *Harriot*, we allude to, as
among those many just now mentioned. Do
we love you? witness we do so yourselves.
How, therefore, can we speak or even think
in any manner of you that accords not with the
love we bear you, when as frequently it happens we are absent from each other. During
such our separation, we consider how much
joy and pleasure fill the room up, when we sit
between you. We repeat within ourselves
those names of *Ann* and *Harriot*. How delightful is the sound of those two words! and
how enchanting they appear when written upon
paper, since they put us in remembrance of the
dear dear little hands that penn'd them, though
when all is said, exclusive of the satisfaction
that results from gazing at your native elegance and interesting figures, you bestow no
favour on us, save that gratitude you manifest
for our poor obligations, and desire to do you
all the good we can : and yet this eagerness has
very narrow limits, and is never so successful
as it wishes. Why then, dearest children, we
are preaching to, why do not you love God?

If

If you did fo, could you at any time, as we have faid already, fpeak, or even think in fuch a manner of him, as accords not with the love you would in that cafe bear him? No, but being in the flefh, or feparated from him, you would frequently confider how much joy and pleafure muft fill up thofe heavenly courts where he difplays his glorious prefence. You would every now and then repeat within yourfelves the name of your creator, friend, and bene-factor. You would every now and then, in fhort, repeat within yourfelves the name of God. How fweet, would you ejaculate, does not that name, above all others, found to our delighted hearing! how enchanting does it not appear when written upon paper, fince it puts us in remembrance of the kindnefs he takes pleafure every day to fhew us! And befides, you would confider that his eagernefs to do fo is not checked by any incapacity within him, or adhering to his nature. Love then God, dear children, your creator, friend, and bene-factor, it will be a fountain for fuch heads of converfation as will fave you from the crime of every thing that looks like idle talk, and much more fo, fallacious and prophane or wicked con-verfation with each other, if the education you

receive

receive could possibly allow us to suppose you would in any manner make yourselves accountable for this last sin.

The text then, literally speaking, may, with great propriety, dear children, be addressed to you. Who, therefore, is ambitious to be called a virtuous child among you, or a child endued with knowledge? let him shew he is so by his conversation. With this admonition we dismiss you. Think not, that the subject of this sermon you have heard, has been a trifling one. Bad conversation surely is a source of vice, that those who are engaged in education should attend to, and suppress the mischiefs of it. May the Almighty, of his grace, succeed their vigilance, and no corrupt communications issue from you. May your lips, your tongue, and every organ of your frame, be dedicated to his service. In the troubles of this life may you experience God your certain refuge. On your death-bed, may he be your hope and consolation, and at last, when that eternity begins to which we all look forward, may he prove your recompence, through Jesus Christ our Lord, &c.

THE

THE HYMN.

OH God of the world, who my tongue did
    firſt frame,
That therewith I might pray, and thy praiſes
    proclaim ;
Let no prophane language my lips e'er diſgrace,
Or oaths, or vain talking, thy preſent debaſe.

But let it thy name extol all day long ;
Thy name the great ſubject, and theme of my
    ſong :
Thy praiſe for paſt goodneſs, ſtill let it record,
And hope that freſh mercies, thy love will
    award.

So thinking of thee, as at all times I ought,
Thro' life I ſhall paſs, pure in deed, word, and
    thought :
While curſing and ſwearing, too many employ ;
Unmov'd, notwithſtanding their ſouls they
    deſtroy.

SERMON

SERMON XXII.

ON LEARNING.

PROVERBS ix. v. 9.

Give inſtruction to a wiſe man, and he will
be yet wiſer.

YES, dear children, and the rule will hold
reſpecting thoſe too of your ſtanding in
the world, for take due notice, that the words,
wiſe man, here introduced by Solomon, when
he informs us that inſtruction given ſuch a one
will make him wiſer, mean a man repleniſhed
with ſuch wiſdom, as the generality of people
loſe ſtill more and more the further they have
travelled on in life from childhood, who inſtead
of willing to take counſel, or receive inſtruction, will be always *arguing* on it. Now a
child's behaviour is not this. inſtead of *arguing*,
he is glad to pay *obedience*. You have heard,
no doubt, that children make much greater
progreſs in whatever they are ſet to learn of

VOL. II. E maſters,

masters, than grown people   And why do
they so? because, however strange you may
consider the expression, they are wiser than
grown people, not because they have a greater
understanding, for, in fact, men's understanding ripens in the same proportion as their
strength increases· but because they are convinced, what little stock of knowledge they
are really possessed of, while grown people
think they have within them an immensity of
knowledge   Hence, were we to give a definition of the thing called wisdom, we should
call it very properly, a conscious knowledge of
our ignorance   Now, who can be more likely to possess this conscious knowledge of their
ignorance, than children? it ensues then,
as such ignorance is the foundation stone
of learning, or first step to knowledge, that
instruction given a wise child will make
him wiser, while a foolish child will, by the
same instruction, grow more foolish.

Chuse, dear children, whether of these different parties you will be enrolled with, whether now, while you are under the tuition of
instructors, you will wish to be considered wise
or foolish : but be sure of this, that on the preference you give to either party, will depend
your

your happinefs or forrow in this life, and that which is to follow. Solomon informs us, that to afk for knowledge, is a fign of previous knowledge in the mind. If it were not, would he have made that choice which is on record of him? Let us give you a detail of this fo celebrated choice, extracted from the firft of Kings. The Lord, as we may gather from the facred writer, when king Solomon was facrificing to him at a place called Gibeon, fhowed himfelf by night, and thus befpoke him, through the medium of a vifion, faying: *afk what I fhall give thee:* and the king made anfwer to the following purport: *Thou haft fhowed great mercy to my father David, in proportion to the truth, integrity of heart, and righteoufnefs with which he walked before thee, and haft added this great kindnefs, namely: that thou gaveft him a fon in his declining years, that might fucceed him on the throne. And yet oh Lord! what am I? nothing but a little child, incapable of governing fo great a multitude as were my father's fubjects. Give thy fervant therefore a judicious and an honeft heart, that he may judge thy people, and difcern between the good and evil.* This was the requeft of Solomon; and as we read, it pleafed the Lord that he had afked this thing; on which ac-

*ount he said, because thou hast required under-
standing, and not length of days, or riches, or
the conquest of thine enemies, I do according to
thy words. I give thee understanding, and the
things thou hast not asked for, namely, wealth
with honor; and if only thou wilt execute my
judgments, I will give thee likewise length of days.*

Thus far the prayer of Solomon, with the
success it met with: such is uniformly the success of those who place their ultimate depend-
ance on the providence of God. He may indeed sometimes deprive them of one blessing,
but he grants them constantly another in its
stead, and if we seek his kingdom, and the
righteousness thereof, we may be sure that
many other blessings will be added to it. Seek
then you God's kingdom and the righteousness
thereof, and in the spirit of that prayer addressed by Solomon to the Almighty, in the book
of WISDOM, the ninth chapter, verse the fourth,
as he did, say *Oh God of my forefathers, give
me wisdom that abideth by thy throne, and cast
me not away, when I request to be received among
the number of thy children.*

Think of this, dear little friends, and fer-
vently pour out your hearts in prayer, that God
would of his mercy grant you wisdom to solicit

at

at his hand that wifdom, which fhall give a
bleffing to the inftruction you receive, fo as to
render you ftill wifer, for as now muft be confeffed the time, in which you may with greateft profit to yourfelves, remember your creator,
fo too now, muft be confeffed the time in
which you may with greateft profit to yourfelves
remember that the bufinefs of your youth is to
become poffeffed of knowledge, or be wife,
while wifdom may bring confolation with it.
for believe us, there is fuch a thing as wifdom,
which interpreted in fuch a manner as it fhould
be, means remorfe of confcience, or at leaft
experience purchafed at a heavy price indeed.
yet ftill, dear children, is it wifdom or experience, and the price, though heavy, cannot be of
greater value than the thing it buys. Such wifdom or experience was the prodigal's, in his re-
pentant ftate. Alas! thofe goods he challeng-
ed as his portion, and which goods the affection
of a father gave up to him, were fo valuable
that he did not fee he was folicitous to leave a
houfe, where even the domeftic fervants had
fuch plenty, but when wifdom or experience,
owing to thofe forrows or diftreffes which were
brought upon him by irregular and vicious
courfes, got admiffion to his heart, he found

E 3 how

how happy it would make him, would his father only condefcend to grant him wages as a
fervant, after as a fon, he had defpifed his
kindnefs. The condition of a hireling fervant,
when compared with that of a beloved fon, was
in reality humiliating, yet with wages he
would hardly die for want, while keeping at a
diftance from his father's houfe, he fhould
infallibly be ftarved to death. The figurative
fenfe of this expreffion, *ftarved to death*, dear
little hearers, underftand, exert your utmoft to
avoid the horror it implies. and granting any
one among you fhould have let too great a portion of his childhood pafs away, without obtain-
ing that degree of learning he might eafily have
gained, let him reflect upon the prodigal, and
imitate his conduct in the fpirit of it, or come
back into the path way of his duty. And let
thofe, who like the prodigal s more duteous
brother, have not hitherto mifufed the feafon of
their childhood, but employed it to the utmoft
of their power in gaining knowledge, ftill continue their affiduous conduct They will find in
future what a permanent foundation they have
all along been laying for their happinefs in this
world, and as elfewhere we have intimated, in
the world that is to come hereafter.

Dear

Dear difciples, you that are thus bleffed by providence with parents, that have where-withal to give you a polite or learned education, we have nothing further, or but very little more, for your attention on the fubject of this fermon, having in fo many paffages of other fermons, fpoken of the duty you are bound in to employ the feafon of your childhood in the acquifition of found learning with polite ac-complifhments, and laid down all the benefits that will refult from fuch found learning and polite accomplifhments in future to you. But you know, there is another portion of the rifing generation, thofe we mean on this occafion, whom the charity of well difpofed and affluent individuals look upon as proper objects to em-ploy itfelf upon, that in a chriftian land they may not live without a chriftian education; and to thefe we would devote the whole re-maining part of our difcourfe. Yes, plants that are particularly watered by the dews of Heaven, fince it is not nature working in the hearts of parents for thofe children which even inftinct teaches them to love, but grace diffufing its exalted influence through the bofoms of good men and women, for thofe children which their charity inftructs them to hold precious,

as

as no lefs proceeding from the hand of the Almighty than themfelves,—fince, we repeat, it
is not nature, but God's grace that prompts
the bofoms of good men and women with that
fpirit of benevolence which every day fupplies
you in fo many quarters of the land, like Dorcas in her charity, with coats and other garments, and which goes beyond the charity of
Dorcas, by annexing to fuch valuable gifts, the
benefit of fchooling, and fure means of knowing God. Yes, infants, we fay, that are particularly watered by the dews of Heaven, weigh
well your happy fortune, and employ the opportunity afforded you in fuch a manner as may
moft accord with the benevolent intention of
your friends. We do not fay, get all the
knowledge you can poffibly pick up, though
that is, in reality, your duty, for when put into
the balance with another duty of much nobler
fort, it rather looks like cunning, as if any one
fhould fay, *I have got fuch or fuch a friend, or
patron, and will make the moft I can of his good
will.* and not *I have got fuch or fuch a friend, or
patron, and will be as grateful as I can for his
good will.* Hence, little ones, you may fee
clearly, that the nobler duty we would recommend, is that of gratitude. Yes, children of
humility,

humility, be grateful for the benefits beftowed upon you Let thofe little hands which were beftowed that you might lift them up to God in prayer for bleffings on yourfelves, be fome-times likewife lifted up for bleffings on your friends. And that your gratitude may never want an object to excite it forcibly within your heart, look often at yourfelves While other children ramble up and down the ftreets, or ftroll along the public roads half naked, and expofed to all the wretchednefs of cold and hunger, you are cloathed with comfortable raiment, and no few of you fupplied with com-fortable food While other children live in ignorance of all things, you are, on the other hand, taught many ufeful matters, and inftruct-ed in your duty firft of all to God, and in the next place to yourfelves We doubt not but you read your Bible, and may very well re-member how the little Jefus, when a child, as moft of you are, every day grew up in wifdom and in favor both with God and man. Re-femble him in this increafe, which you may do with eafe, fo great is the attention paid you¹ and endeavour, each among you, to be that *w fo child* the text alludes to, *who, provided he is taught, will grow yet wifer.* Pay obedience

E 5

to your parents, be fubmiffive to your teachers, and as all of you fhould both begin and end the day upon your knees before the Almighty,. make it conftantly your prayer that he would blefs your effoits to be grateful for thofe clothes and that inftruction you receive, of thofe who never knew you, being taught not only how to read, which would fuffice that you might know God's will and pleafure, but even wiite and caft accounts, in which, if you arrive at any tolerable fkill, that is, if you are ready, with your pen, and good arithmeticians, you may be affured of gaining in this land of trade,, a comfortable livelihood. And, little maids, we have a word too of encouragement for you. Your futuie fituation will be that, we take it, of domeftic fervants, which the feveral arts of houfewifery you are inftructed in, will fully qualify you for   In time, when you are fettled in the world, we doubt not you will hear it faid, that *fervice is not an inheritance*, and more fuch ftuff. But be affured that thefe expreffions come from none but indolent and worthlefs fervants, who, it muft be granted, are fo often changing places, that they cannot poffibly ex-perience an inheritance in feivice. You will find your intereft in never quitting that firft

place,

place, to which the will of providence may
call you ; and that nothing may enfue to make
you quit it, fhew yourfelves both diligent and
faithful to the feveral families employing you ;
and then you will be able to retain your fervice, for be fure of this, that miftreffes and
mafters love themfelves fo well, that they will
never wantonly difmifs a ufeful fervant. Then
will you be able alfo to fave money, and fo find
your fervice *is* an actual inheritance. In fine,
remember Jofeph, whofe fidelity and diligence
promoted him from fervitude to be a lord in
Egypt, but particularly recollect, that Jofeph
had the fear of God before his eyes, in which
if you take care to imitate him, you will find
your recompenfe can never fail you in futurity,
though here you fhould remain unable to obtain
a comfortable maintenance, which is fuppofing
what can hardly ever be the cafe.

Oh father of the world, write thefe great
truths upon the heart of fuch as we have laft
been preaching to, and fill the firft with proper
notions of their happy fituation, fo that they
may turn it to their benefit in future life, by
acquifition of that learning, which their anxious
and indulgent parents pay to have them taught.
Let the folicitude of thefe in favour of all thofe

proceed-

proceed'rg from their loins, admonifh them of
other children, who, at leaft, fhould not be
deftitute of a religious education, and accordingly may they conduct themfelves in fuch a
manner, that when finally the time is come for
gathering up their feet into the bed, as Jacob
did, and having, as he had, their children
gathered round them, they may every one have
caufe to fay · Dear children, I have always
looked on gold as refufe in comparifon of you,
which gold I have at no time fpared, when
called on to fupport, to educate, and clothe
the children born to others, and who, doubtlefs,
looked on gold as refufe in comparifon of them.
Fear nothing, therefore, for, dear children,
though I die, God will be always gracious to
you And this thought that fhould be confolation and fupport to you, now fweetens that
unhappy cup which I muft drink, obedient to
God's will and pleafure, fince the moment of
our feparation from each other is arrived. God
grant, dear children, that your parents may, in
dying, have this confolation, for the fake of
Jefus Chrift, &c.

THE

THE HYMN.

WITH my whole heart, I give thee thanks,
    Oh Lord, that I was born
Here, in a country, that such arts
    And sciences adorn.

Those arts and sciences to know,
    Let me my efforts aim,
And may my mind intensely glow
    With learning's ardent flame.

While, since around my dwelling place,
    So many I discern,
Whose parents have not wherewithal
    To pay, that they may learn,

Let me to these, when ask'd, some part
    Of my scant havings give,
That in thy volume they may read
    What it contains, and live.

SERMON

SERMON XXIII.

ON WHIT-SUNDAY.

ACTS II. V. 4.

They were all filled with the holy ghost.

WE have said already, little children, what we say once more, that every miracle performed by the Redeemer, did not merely set forth his divinity, or power, but was instructive too. Accordingly, by this which we shall now consider, we are taught, that destitute of aid and succour from above, whatever we may undertake, no matter how important to God's glory, we are weak, and cannot possibly succeed therein. Of this, our Lord's apostles were convinced, for how could they be unconvinced when he had given them such instructions on this head? And here we enter on our present subject, namely. the descent of what is called the holy ghost on Jesus Christ's apostles, which he called *the promise of*

the

the father, its defcent, we fay, into the hearts
of thofe who were felected from the reft of men
to publifh the religion of their bleffed mafter.

In our Eafter-funday's exhortation, we ir-
formed you that our Saviour, being rifen from
the dead, appeared to his difciples feveral times
alive, and in his proper perfon, not as what
we call a ghoft or fpirit, but made up of flefh
and blood. Of this, do all the four Evangelifts
inform us; after which, St. Luke alone, who
wrote the *acts of the apoftles*, re-affumes the hif
tory, and gives us a detail of fome few circumftances that took place before a cloud concealed
Chrift Jefus from the fight of his difciples, at
the moment he was taken up to heaven.

The words of the Evangelift in fubftance are
as follow: " Jefus Chrift for forty days toge-
" ther, being feen of his difciples, and at times
" too eating with them, ordered that they fhould
" not quit Jerufalem, but wait the *promife of his*
" *father which*, faid he, *I have already made you.*
" Upon this, they afked him, if, as confequential
" to his refurrection, he intended to reftore im-
" mediately the kingdom to God's people? But
" he anfwered, it was not for them to know
" the times or feafons, which his father had
" thought fit to put in his own power. You
" fhall

" shall however, all of you, continued he,
" have power, when once the holy ghost is
" come upon you, and shall then become my
" witnesses, not only in Jerusalem, but likewise
" in Judea and Samaria, and in every distant
" region of the earth. And when," says our
evangelist, " he had said this, and while too
" they were looking at him, he was taken from
" them by a cloud. While they were looking
" steadfastly towards heaven, as he was rising,,
" lo two men stood by them, robed in white,
" who said: *ye men of Galilee, why stand ye gaz-*
" *ing thus? This Jesus, who is taken from you*
" *into heaven, shall in like manner come again,*
" *as ye have seen him go.* On this, the compa-
" ny of his disciples left the mount of Olives :
" (for Christ met them for the last time there,
" when he ascended), and came back into Jeru-
" salem, where they assembled in the upper cham-
" ber of a house, to pass the time in prayer. In
" such an occupation were they met together till
" the day of Pentecost, (that is the fiftieth after
" Easter), was arrived, when of a sudden there
" was heard a sound as some sort like a rushing
" mighty wind, that filled the house where they
" were sitting. And they saw twelve cloven
" tongues, resembling tongues of fire, that light-
                                              " ed

" ed upon every one among them, and that mo-
" ment were they all replenished with the holy spi-
" rit, and began to speak in other languages.
" This wonder could not fail to bring a multitude
" together, who were then residing at Jerusalem,
" devout and pious men of every nation under hea-
" ven, who flocking thither, were confounded
" when they heard the apostles unexpectedly ad-
" dress them in the language each was used to
" speak, and though the apostle Peter, previous to
" his master s crucifixion, as already we have
" shown you, was so very fearful that he durst not
" openly avow himself a follower of Christ Je-
" sus, yet addressing now this multitude, he
" taxed them with the murder of his master,
" whom, said he, you *wickedly* have put to
" death . but God, as he continued, had al-
" ready raised him from the dead, because it
" was not possible the grave should hold him
" long within it   Having said thus much, he
" turned their observation on the prophecy of
" David, with regard to Jesus Christ, and
" proved that he whom they had crucified in
" this unrighteous manner, was the person spo-
" ken of by David upon which," says the
historian, " they were pricked in heart,
" and said to Peter and his fellows, what
                                    " would

" would you advife us to ?   When the apoftle
" bade them firft of all repent, and afterward be
" every one baptifed with water, in the name
" of Jefus Chrift, for the remiffion of their fins,
" which, if they did, they fhould receive the
" holy fpirit likewife.   With this falutary
" counfel they complied, and there were added,
" upon that occafion, to the twelve difciples, up-
" wards of three thoufand fouls, that afterward
" increafed in number daily, by the admiffion of
" as many as were deftined to believe. '

This, little hearers, is the hiftory abridged of
that tranfaction we are now affembled to com-
memorate or fpeak of, the defcent upon our
Saviour's twelve difciples of that fpirit, which
illuminated and emboldend them to publifh,
firft, among the Jews, the doctrine of that bleffed perfon they had crucified, and afterward,
among the Gentiles likewife, which great labour was referved particularly for the miniftra-
tion of St. Paul, who hitherto had not appeared
among the number of the twelve difciples, but
even perfecuted fuch as followed their new
faith.

Efpecially from this apoftle therefore, fhall
we draw thofe arguments that are to fill the part
remaining of this exhortation : from St. Paul,
who,

who in more paſſages than one of his epiſtles, ſpeaking of the holy ſpirit, ſent at Pentecoſt to men, inſtead of calling it God's ſpirit, ſays; the ſpirit of Chriſt Jeſus. thus, in Romans, *God hath ſent the ſpirit of his ſon into your hearts.* The comforter by Jeſus promiſed, therefore, is himſelf, but manifeſted in another form, and conſequently every thing he did referred to Jeſus Chriſt. That is to ſay, he came among us, firſt to glorify the Saviour, which the Saviour ſaid he would, thus in St John the ſixteenth chapter : When the ſpirit, he remarks, *of truth is come, he will guide you into all truth, for he ſhall not witneſs of himſelf, but whatſoever he ſhall hear that ſhall he ſpeak ; and he will ſhow you things to come. He ſhall glorify me ; for he ſhall receive of mine and ſhall ſhow it you.*

From hence it follows, therefore, that redemption by the death of Jeſus Chriſt, a work exceedingly confined in point of time and ſpace, would have been incomplete, but for the preſence afterward of his moſt holy ſpirit, which in all its operations was unlimited in point of time and ſpace, and with which ſpirit the apoſtles, as our text informs us, were all filled, that by their mediation it might glorify Chriſt Jeſus, that is, make him known, for men did not in any

manner

manner know him, otherwise than in the flesh.
But all our happiness must flow from an acquaintance with his spirit. What then came
to pass upon the day of Pentecost? The spirit
of that body which had suffered death for
men's past sins, was sent to teach us how we
might avoid all future sins, and the design of
God in our redemption, then became complete.

And whence could this proceed? Whence
dear disciples, if not caused by the immediate
inspiration of this holy spirit? The corporal
presence of the Saviour upon earth, as we have
said already, though a part, was not the greatest
of redemption, for the spirit, sent into men's
hearts in many regions of the globe, was to
perform that work, which the redeemer's per-
sonal appearance, in one region of the globe,
did not perform. This truly was to glorify
Christ Jesus, as himself had prophecied should
happen, saying, he shall take of mine, and shew
it to you.

But again, and secondly, the holy spirit came
among us not alone to glorify Christ Jesus, but to
ripen or perfectionate the doctrine he had planted by his death, in other words dear children,
to build up the law of love delivered in his
gospel.

For

For till then, the rigorous law of Mofes had fubfifted · but it loft its efficacy by the operation of the holy fpirit, and a new one was eftablifhed in its ftead--eftablifhed by the comforter , which law was therefore one of love, becaufe it could not be confiftent with a comforter to fix another rigorous law. Accordingly, St. Paul informs his brethren in Galatia, that the fpirit fhows itfelf in love, *whofe fruit*, he fays, *is love, joy, peace.* And this is the redeemer's fpirit, for *a new commandment*, are his words, *I give you, that ye love each other, as myfelf have loved you.* And on this account, has he engraved the law within us, *upon flefhly tables of the heart*, and not on ftone Herein was love, the love, Chrift Jefus recommended to mankind, himfelf omitted not to practife. Now, dear little hearers, love has two effects, for it impoverifhes him that gives it, and enriches the receiver. and accordingly, St. Paul addreffes the Corinthians in this manner: *You all know the grace of Jefus Chrift, that notwithftanding he was rich, yet did he bring himfelf for your fake to be poor ; that by his poverty you might be rich.*

Herein we fay is love, and yet by no means fuch a love as for the firft time was then manifefted to the world. but a continuation of that

love,

love, though with addition, which has conftantly been poured upon men's heads from the beginning : for to gain their hearts, God previoufly appointed every creature to their ufe, and
for four thoufand years and upward, gave them
feafons, with the former and the latter rain, to
fertilize the earth : but notwithftanding fo much
love in our behalf, fin ftill continued to infult
or grieve his holy fpirit, which, that he might
put away, and raife us to the dignity of virtue,
he confented that his fon fhould fuffer death on
our account, and yet, his fon, by fuffering, did
not put away our fin. What then was to be done?
Was he to give up our unyielding hearts? No.
he refolved, on any terms, to gain us, and adopted the ftupendoufly affectionate intention of bef-
towing nothing lefs upon us than himfelf, of
entering, as St Paul expreffes it, into our hearts,
and though defpifed while he fojourned among
us, of returning as a comforter to teach thofe
individuals whom his death had not inftructed.

If then it be fo, muft we not yield to fuch a
prodigy of love? We muft. let us, dear children then, by way of moral to this exhortation,
in the firft place, fpeak to you, and fay, fince
everlafting love has been fo great, be it your part,
in thefe your early years, in the fimplicity of
childhood,

childhood, to evince an equal love, by doing
what the candour of your artless nature qualifies
you to perform, and *that* without an effort, as
God's law requires : for *if you love me, keep,* fays
Jefus, *my commandments.* In the obfervation of
this precept, will your love confift; for as he
adds, *you are my friends, if you perform what I
command you.* And what motive are you not
all bound in, to obey this precept of your Saviour ? In your catechifm, you are every one
inftructed to love God, and yet the laws of God
were publifhed to mankind in *thunders,* and, as
Mofes tells us, *lightnings,* while the mount,
from which God fpoke, was burning with an
awful fire, but Jefus Chrift, dear friends, when
he delivered you his law, affectionately took you
in his arms, embraced, and bleffed you. Show
then, you poffefs that love, which he has taught
your little hearts, and be it feen by all you
have to do with, in the effects it conftantly produces ; always recollecting that to fhow it muft
be an effect of the redeemer's fpirit ; for the
fpirit is to teach you all things, and your innocence, believe me, does not render you lefs welcome pupils. May the fpirit therefore of our
Lord engraft upon your prefent and involuntary
innocence, a future innocence made manifeft in
all

l

all your actions This, dear children, is our prayer in your behalf, and for ourself, may, as Elifha faid, a double portion of this fpirit fall upon us, that while teaching others, we may not be, as St. Paul expreffes it, a caft-away. Give, give me, therefore, holy fpirit, that one needful gift of grace, not that of working miracles, fince it redouds not to falvation either in the teacher or the taught, but of inftruction in the way of righteoufnefs, not that of language, but humility, not that of healing bodily diforders but directing, in a ftate of innocence, the ductile difpofition of thofe heirs to heaven I am addreffing Give me, (to be brief) the fimple fpirit, the true wifdom of that chriftianity my Saviour taught, and banifh from me the falfe fpirit of thofe politics which make men cunning for the world. Give me the fpirit thou beftoweft on thine elect, the comforter thou fendeft to teach us all things, my fure feal in this life, and my glory in the life to come. Hear too thy fervant, in behalf not only of himfelf, with thofe affembled round him, but in favour of mankind in general, and oh fovereign creator, the defcent of whofe moft holy fpirit on the apoftles we are this day met to celebrate, enlighten alfo us. Thou, that particularly art the father of the

poor,

poor, and the difpenfer of celeftial bleffings con-
fecrate the place in which thy worfhippers in
every quarter of the globe are met together, for
through thee, we find repofe in toil, refrefhment
in the hour of pain, and confolation in diftrefs.
Remove the ftony from our hearts, heal all our
maladies, and clofe the wounds up of our fin.
Give every one among us an affurance of Salvation, here below. With that affurance, calm
the troubled moment of our foul's departure
from its tenement of duft, and realize the long-
ings of our faith in future, when with thee, the
fon, and fpirit, we enjoy eternal happinefs in
Heaven. Amen.

THE HYMN.

COME everlafting fpirit;
Bright power, from heaven fwift gliding,
For Jefus' fake,
Our bodies make
Thy temple to refide in,

Thy glorious infpiration,
If to our prayer 'tis given,
    Shall from within
    Expel our fin,
And make us fit for Heaven.

Come then, and fill our bofoms,
So henceforth, fhall we never
    While we have breath,
    By fin earn death,
Since born to live for ever.

With faith our hearts poffefs then,
Tho now by guilt infected,
    And teach us, too,
    How we may do
Thofe works from men expected.

SERMON XXIV.

ON CHARITY.

Whence should we have so much bread in the wilderness as to fill so great a multitude?

THIS was the question put to Christ by his disciples, after he had manifested his compassion and desire to feed the multitude that had come forth to hear him in the wilderness, and were so far from home that, if dismissed without refreshment, he was fearful they would faint, as he expressed it, by the way: and his proceeding, both before and after he occasioned this enquiry, is an admirable model for the tender hearted to pursue, and likewise such a model as is capable of imitation by mankind, almost as soon as they are furnished with a heart to think, or with a hand to give:—for what is charity?

It

It is a difpofition to be kind, and do our neighbour all the good we can. If, therefore, we poffefs this difpofition, though we never have the opportunity or means of being kind, or doing good, we are in God's idea charitable. Charity, confidered in this fenfe, dear children, is a virtue of the heart, and you are capable thereof, becaufe you have a heart, and *that* too fuch a kind and good one! Witnefs for the truth of this, thofe eyes that always ftart with tears, at the recital or account of any mournful ftory. but we will not here pay any further compliment to the fimplicity and lovelinefs of children. We proceed to our immediate fub-ject, and inform you that Chrift Jefus, juft be-fore he had been afked the queftion in our text, had been performing miracles, and teaching (we may naturally think) a multitude of people; in which actions, he performed the work of cha-rity, according to that definition we have juft now given of it, namely, as a virtue of the heart.

But in the next place, charity confifts in be-ing actually kind and doing good, and taken in this fenfe, it is a virtue of the hand. Now all of us, dear little friends, have not an equal opportunity of being charitable in this way; though

though few are totally deprived of power to help their fellow-creatures. God, however, in his goodnefs to give all his children the rewards of charity, confidered even as a virtue of the hand, does not·require us to beftow upon the needy fuch or fuch a fum of money to relieve them, but as much as we can fpare, for you have furely read of that poor widow, whofe two mites, which were together only worth one farthing, were more acceptable as a charity to God, than many rich mens' gifts, and you have likewife furely read, that if you meet a weary and exhaufted traveller by the way, and cheerfully fupply him with a cup of water in the coldeft feafon of the year, provided you have nothing likelier to revive his fainting flame, you fhall in no cafe fail of your reward. And here we fay again, that Jefus Chrift, immediately on being afked the queftion mentioned in our text, proceeded to fupply the bodily neceffities of thofe about him, who he feared would perifh, if difmiffed without a meal, in doing which, he practifed charity according to the latter definition given of it, namely, as a virtue of the hand.

But here it may be afked; why God fhould have been fo folicitous to make this virtue prac-

ticable

ticable by mankind in every state of life?—
Because it is a virtue which unless we have, all
others are of no effect. *If,* says the Apostle, *I
have all the knowledge of an angel, with sufficient
faith to root up mountains ; and though possibly I
were to give my body to be burnt, and all my goods
to feed the poor,* in this he speaks of charity as
being nothing but a virtue of the hand, *and have
not charity,* that virtue which is seated in the
bosom, *I am nothing.* Could he possibly, dear
children, more convincingly have shown the
worthlessness of every virtue, unaccompanied
by that we recommend at present ?—What is
this, but saying charity alone shall give us any
claim to Heaven?

But there is something else ; for the Apostle
puts a difference between that charity which
would suggest the sale of all our goods to feed
the poor, which is a virtue, as defined already,
of the hand, and real charity : in other words,
he tells us that the virtue of the hand is nothing,
while the virtue of the heart is that alone entitled to the praise and recompence of charity.

Hear this, this flattering explanation, little
ones, that form a rising generation, and conceive the providence and wisdom of God's love.

While

While men and women, (thofe we mean that
are grown up to years of reafon and reflexion),
fhall not merit future happinefs without the exertion of at leaft three virtues, *faith*, as the Apoftle tells us, *hope*, and *charity*, that future happinefs
in you fhall be the crown of charity alone. Hear
likewife that this virtue, with regard to you, is
much more fimplified than in the hands and bofom of your elders we all know it is. The virtue
of the hand is not by you in general to be practifed, at that time of life, when you are void of
property. The virtue of the heart alone is
therefore called for, and fo gracious is the Almighty, that at prefent you are heirs to Heaven
by virtue of your imbecility or weaknefs.
Who could have imagined that when God firft
made the world, he had employed fuch care
and fo ethought for the benefit of thofe that
fhould but fpring to life, but juft fhoot forth
their tender leaves, and die before fufficient
time was granted them to bring forth fruit?
Well, therefore, if the cafe be fo, might Jefus
Chrift inform us that *of you*, that is *belonging to
you*, is God's kingdom.

There is fomething, little ones, however, we
would fain remark before we point you out the
-way in which it will behove you to acquit your-

felves of this great duty : namely, not the providence alone and wifdom of your heavenly father, but his tendernefs as well.   The generality among you know how far the tendernefs of
thofe who are your earthly parents, goes ; and
yet, dear little ones, they fometimes have their
favourites , lavifh of their love to them, they
treat their other children rather harfhly , and
the reafon of it is, becaufe the meafure of affection in their heart is limited, and therefore, if
they fhow themfelves profufely kind to one or
two, it muft be unavoidably at the expence of
all their other children.   In a manner, as the pa-
triarch Ifaac did, they muft give reafon to foms
little one, lefs favoured than another in the family, to afk them if they have one only blefling
to beftow   but God is infinite in bleffings , and
with him no favourite is felected, fo that any
others of his children are lefs kindly treated at
his hands.   And yet, as you muft likewife
know, thofe parents who are' fo unjuft,—unjuft
we call it, though their conduct is occafioned
rather by the frailty than perverfity of human
nature,—fo unjuft, we fay, as to felect a favourite, upon that account, incline not to abate
a little of the duty all their other children owe
them ? rather, may we fay, that in their parti-
                                                   ality

ality for one, they commonly tie down the reft to harder terms ; and often fome of thofe lefs favoured fhall have reafon to complain, that for no other reafon very likely than becaufe they have a lefs engaging outfide or appearance, they are forced to undergo humiliation, and more-over have fuch duties laid upon them as they are not able to accomplifh : but with God, there can be nothing to lament of fuch a nature. His capacious bofom can make every one a favou-rite, and the duty he expects from every indi-vidual of his numerous family, is in proportion to his means of being duteous. God, although by virtue of his greatnef., he has every right and title to unlimited obedience, forms fuch expec-tations as proclaim our incapacity to ferve him, rather than his wifh of being ferved as if he were our mafter.

Children, therefore, in your youth, let us ex-hort you to the exercife of fo fublime a virtue; and as far as in its exercife the heart is occu-pied, be followers of Jefus Chrift, no lefs con-firmed and fettled in your principles, than if you had been walking in the paths of chriftianity, a long life through, for you may do fo, having, as we faid before, a heart. But with refpect to charity, confidered as a virtue of the hand,

F 5

though

though much you cannot do, yet ftill you may
do fomething. *Whence fhall we buy bread that.*
thefe may eat? So fay you in your hearts, when
any object of calamity, when, for example, any
child of forrow ftands before you—" Whence
" fhall I find means that fuch a one may be
" relieved? Have I a pittance to beftow from
" that, comparatively fpeaking, plenteous ftock,
" which the indulgent bounty of my parents
" gives me weekly? Have I, be it nothing
" but a morfel of hard bread to give? I muft
" give fomething. Sure then I can hold him
" out a cup of water. Take, poor man or
" woman—take, poor child, this trifle from a
" hand that has not much in its poffeffion to
" beftow upon you, but from one whofe heart,
" his parents tell him, fhould be always in a
" difpofition to fhow kindnefs, and do all the
" good he can · take this flight charity, and do
" the giver that much greater charity, of ear-
" neftly imploring that God's goodnefs would
" keep up within him a compaffionate and feel-
" ing heart, not lefs on all occafions than on
" this, increafe with my increafing means that
" feeling or compaffion, and give larger fcope
" thereto, by fhewing me the bleffednefs, as
" well as pleafure I fhall reap, if I forego my
" own

" own enjoyments to feed others in diſtreſs.
" 'Take it, and may God's grace inſpire ſome
" richer perſon to relieve your wants."

It might not be a piece of counſel any ways
miſplaced, dear children, if at preſent you
ſhould limit the benevolent effuſions of your
little hearts to children like yourſelves. Perhaps you would not do much good, ſhould you
beſtow your trifle upon other objects, but
with them your charity will be effectual; and,
not only *that*, but meritorious likewiſe: for of
thoſe who having ſtrength to work, are often
found ſoliciting the hand of charity, how many
might we not point out purſuing ſuch an occupation as a trade, if more deplorable to hint,
they have not, by their crimes, contributed to
bring down poverty upon themſelves, while, by
their crimes, they are ſtill kept in ſuch a ſtate;
and this we do not ſay to check the feelings of
your charity, but, on the other hand, to put
you in a way by which your charity may be attended with a greater bleſſing ſtill; while you
beſtow your mite for the relief of thoſe who are
not old enough as yet to have before hand made
a trade of begging charity, or who, by any
crimes now perpetrated, do not keep themſelves
in a precarious, needy ſtate, or who, by crimes

of old committed, have not been reduced to
their unhappy fituation. With refpect to
them, it may be literally faid, they are the
offspring of humility; for many of them hardly can do more than lifp the language of their
wants, but charity, dear little friends, that
charity which aids their bodily neceffities, and
which, St. Paul informs us, *hopeth all things,*
will incline you to fuppofe their hearts will, at
a future period, glow with gratitude for the
affiftance you may hold them out from time to
time. In fhort, they are unable to befriend
themfelves; and, in fuch fituation, they re-
mind us of thofe waters, upon which all cafting, as the fcripture fays, their bread, fhall
find it after many days are paffed. Let us con-
jure you then, dear little hearers, that whenever you may hear, or fee, a child implore
your pity, you would not content yourfelves
with faying, at the impulfe of that gentle difpofition which we truft you have, " poor child,
" be clothed and fed, and have your wants fup-
" plied." That wifh, no doubt, will be ac-
-cepted by a god of charity, from fuch as ftand
in need of help themfelves; but you, within
whofe parents' houfes, and about whofe lovely
perfons every thing looks gay, fhould add, to
contem-

contemplative charity, an active liberality, however inconfiderable it may be. And which a-
mong you, at a future period, will be parents,
having little ones yourfelves? I look no great
way forward, and obferve you on a dying bed,
attended by thofe little ones about you, every
one in tears. "I die," the feeble parent fays;
but oh, what joy, if you can add, "yet God,
"dear children, will be gracious to you, for
"my fake; fince early trained to acts of charity,
"when I was even little, did I aid the poor,
"nor ever faw the wounded Jew, and paffed
"him on the other fide."—We finifh our difcourfe, and, in the laft place, fpeak to you,

Poor children, who, by reafon of the negligence, or vice, for which your parents are ac-
cufable, feem born into the world, not as the
offspring you fhould be, of peace, but, in fome
fort, predeftined to the curfe. You fuffer for
the fins, alas! of others, and pay down the
penalty of their mifdeeds, deprived, as frequently you are, of food, of raiment, and that
education which comprifes the fure means of
knowing God But be at length of comfort;
for the dawn of charity is breaking forth in
your behalf, and lighting the whole land, fince
God put gracious thoughts into mens' hearts;

and

and now that facred day which fhould be fpent
in the Creatoi's fervice, but which hitherto has
been allotted, as it were, for piophanation,
greater than the other fix, is, by degrees, becoming facied to the pious purpofe of diffufing
fome flight knowledge, with the means of
knowing God, into your tender minds. Think
not your fituation is deplorable , and, that you
may not think it fo, confider that the mifery of
fuch a multitude of people as infeft the public
ftreets, has either been occafioned by the want of
fuch a bleffing in their childhood, as we truft you
will have fhoitly, if at prefent you poffefs it not,
or by their negligence in profiting thereby , and
know, that after fuch a bleffing has been held
you out, if you continue deftitute and wretched,
the whole fault will be your own , fince you
will then have all the means afforded you, by
which you may become acquainted, as the
fcripture fays, with God.

And as for you, dear little friends, of better
fortune in the woild, here prefent, we conclude
with offering up our humble prayers to God.
Oh, father of mankind, give this increafing family of thine the grace to recollect, that naked
as they came into the world, fo naked muft
they quit it too: and if thy providence fhould,

in their riper years, decree them more than
what is neceffary for life's wants, let them
employ at leaft fome portion of the overplus,
in actions of unfeigned religion and humility,
in vifiting the fatherlefs and widow, while they
keep themfelves unfpotted from the world: but
if that providence, as often for wife purpofes it
does, fhould change the pleafing promife of
their prefent fituation, and reduce them to a
ftate of toil for their fupport, or throw them as
dependants on the charitable few, endow them
with that refignation which can only be the
bleffed produce of thy grace, and may they be
perfuaded they are fet apart, as fufferers, having nothing in this life, that in a future life
they may become poffeffed of all things. Hear
us, we befeech thee, for the fake of Jefus
Chrift, &c.

THE HYMN.

THOUGH with an angel's tongue I fpeak,
  And every fcience know,
Though I have faith that hills could plunge
  Into the depths below;

But

But if in deed, in word, and thought,
I have not Charity, I'm nought.

   Though I should rush into the flames,
      And fell my worldly store
  The deftitute to feed, and give
      Till I had left no more,
Yet without Charity, or love,
I'm nothing in God's fight above.

   Charity does not barely feek
      By law to claim its own:
Charity's ever kind, and ne'er
      Into wild paffion's thrown.
Bears all things, and of every man;
Thinks, hopes, and trufts, the beft it can.

   So excellent is Charity,
      That thofe whereof 'tis one,
  FAITH, HOPE, and CHARITY, by which
      All virtuous acts are done.
Great in themfelves are, yet above,
All fhall be done away but LOVE.

                SERMON

SERMON XXV.

ON A CHOICE OF BOOKS.

2 TIMOTHY, III. V. 15.

From a child thou haft known the holy fcriptures, which are able to make thee wife unto falvation, through faith, which is in Chrift Jefus.

WHAT, dear children, can be more ex-preffive than the human countenance? What more engaging than the youthful? Not that countenance which is fet off by the fuper-fluous ornaments of art or ftudy; but that countenance which, if fuch epithet may be allowed, the œconomical, though not penuri-ous, hand of nature has embellifhed; not that countenance which is concealed beneath a var-nifh of fuch colours as tend rather to disfigure than adorn the unaffected grace of beauty, but that countenance which glows, in every region of it, with the ruby of the rifing fun, or is fet off with all that filver mildnefs, and as fome conceive it greater beauty, of the midnight moon.

moon. In fhort, what more delightful than
that countenance which is impreffed with innocence? While other beauty kindles, what in
fome fort may be called, an interefted love; a
love to which the generality of thofe who cherifh it refign themfelves, from fomething of a
wifh within their bofoms, to exalt the fenfe
they have of pleafure, by the fole poffeffion of
fuch beauty, this awakens, in the heart of thofe,
before whofe eye it paffes, a difinterefted love;
a love, to which, without exception, fuch as
cherifh it refign themfelves, from fomething of
a wifh within their bofoms, to forget their own
enjoyments, and inftead, which is a greater
matter of enjoyment, do their little charmer all
the good they can.

This wifh, endearing children, they who
know your preacher will affert is in *his* heart.
Accuftomed, from his own firft childhood, to
be very often with you, and partaking, in your
company, of a delicious feaft, which never
palls upon the appetite, he has habituated his
fenfations to the relifh of thofe charms, which
neither heighten vanity on one fide, nor create difguft upon the other, and, God's providence be praifed for all things! fuch has been
the joy experienced by him, from fo fweet an
                                        intercourfe,

intercourfe, that life has been by no means
that oppreffive weight to him, which fome in-
heritors of forrow think it. The delight and
fatisfaction thus experienced by him from this
intercourfe, fo grateful to his nature, has not
been a feed unfruitful in its confequences; he
has fought occafions of evincing fomething like
the fruit of gratitude, for fuch delight and fatisfaction, he has not, in fhort, evinced a bar-
ren love within him; he has parted cheerfully
with no fmall portion of his pittance in the
world, that he might fhow the fenfe he had of
obligations laid upon him, and which pittance,
very likely, prudence would have told him to
put by, as fome provifion for the feafon of old
age. At no time has he feen before him an
ingenuous countenance, but he has conftantly
combined therewith a wifh, and not that only,
but an ardour likewife to delight the bofom of its
owner. Men that read good books, rife up
from fuch an entertainment better, or more
pleafed, than when they firft fat down to have
the improvement or the pleafure of their entertainment, and the cafe of fuch has been, dear
children, in fome fort, your preacher's. Your
ingenuous countenances were thofe books where
he could fee intelligible traces drawn upon them;

they

they have always ſtruck him, as it were, like
maps with goodly countries. He has conſtantly
ſet down well pleaſed to glean the information
they afforded, and has riſen from that ſtudy, as
he ſhould have done if he had been invited to a
feaſt,—that is to ſay, with kindly notions of
the founder.

But in theſe laſt lines, as you will ſee, we
have anticipated our deſign, or rather let you
into an acquaintance with our ſubject, while we
did not mean to do ſo; proper books, of which
we mean to treat in this diſcourſe. . Your
countenances have appeared to us good books:
this has been ſaid already, and is now repeated:
and why ſo, dear children ? Why good books?
By reaſon of the innocence impreſſed upon them.
They who ſtudy, by their looks, to pleaſe the
ſouls or underſtandings of beholders, vainly will
conſult a looking-glaſs, in vain will they endeavour to compoſe their features at the toilet.
Pleaſe the eye they may, indeed, by ſuch a
mode; but even then their triumph will be
only for an evening; the laborious taſk muſt
daily be begun anew, and every time they have
recourſe thereto, it will not be ſo proſperous as
it was the time before   Art, you have heard
from thoſe who uſe the figurative ſtyle in ſpeech

or

or writing, may be looked upon as nature's handmaid; and when once the miſtreſs loſes her aſcendency or influence in a human frame, which is the caſe when age inſenſibly ſteals on it, the attendant likewiſe will begin to fail in her alacrity of ſervice · but that innocence, dear little ones, which conſtantly gives greater bright-neſs to the vivid colours on the cheek in child-hood, ſhall improve as you advance in years or underſtanding, and depends not on the help-ing hand of an attendant. We all come into the world with that diſeaſe which, generally ſpeaking, is to end us, therefore, generally ſpeaking too, does the diſeaſe grow ſtronger with our ſtrength; and though it be againſt our inclination or deſire to die, we nurſe or cheriſh it affectionately: ſo too is the innocence of our firſt years an inmate or companion we are born with, and which certainly, in future, will ap-prove itſelf the means of our eternal and un-changed exiſtence; while that innocence, if we but nurſe or cheriſh it, ſhall grow ſtill ſtronger as our ſtrength increaſes. Nurſe or cheriſh then this innocence, if you have any wiſh of being permanently beautiful; for if you ſeek upon the countenance of thoſe now ſunk into the vale of years, and who were formerly acknowledged charming, hardly will you fee a trace remaining of their beauty. It has perifhed in the wrecks of that devouring time which in the firft place takes away the brilliancy of every object, and at laft the very object. Had they toiled as earneftly in the more eafy labour of pre-ferving their firft innocence, it would not, any more than other gifts proceeding from the hand of Heaven, have left them in the time of their decay.

But having fomewhat deviated from our fub-ject, we return; and, fince in this difcourfe we are to give you fome inftructions on fuch books as may be fitting for you, we enquire what fort of books you are to chufe from the immenfity of thofe that libraries abound with? Such, we anfwer, as will not conduce to alter or cor-rupt your innocence. Now, as already we have faid, the countenace is that peculiar region where this innocence difplays itfelf, fo likewife is the countenance that part on which bad books produce an alteration, in thofe blufhes they fpread over it, before, with their infection, they corrupt the heart. From obfervations, may we every one refolve the queftion, as you recol-lect, juft now propounded, of our choice from the immenfity of books, with which the gene-rality

1ality of libraries abound ; for as that innocence which marks the cheek of children, is a gift proceeding from the treafure-houfe or ftores of God, it follows that fuch books are moft adapted to preferve that innocence, as moft relate to God. This is a full and perfect anfwer to the queftion ; and thofe books, dear little ones, you are to fix your choice on, that inculcate one or other of thofe duties God commands us to perform ; fome action of compaffion he delights in, and the like. We know indeed, that children cannot always rivet their attention to religious books ; nor do we therefore recommend that fuch fhould be for ever in their little hands. Variety delights the mind ; and he that thinks a child fhould not expect it, thinks the infant mind fhould be more fettled and fedate, than that of far lefs volatile adolefcence or youth, and likewife of compofed and grave old age, that, as experience fhows us, can unbends itfelf upon occafions by a fhifting of the fcene, and will not to be tied down to contemplate inceffantly upon no more than one fole object : therefore by variety fhould every prudent teacher undertake to captivate his pupil ; and fuppofing, what is not the cafe among us, that a love of fuch variety fhould be a weaknefs

in

in the underſtanding, take advantage of that
weakneſs, and employ it to the benefit of its poſ-
ſeſſor. Hence, what follows? Nothing favourable to the cauſe of thoſe who would not heſi-
tate to put a vicious or improper book into the
hands of children ; for aſſuredly, the ſtate of
learning in the land is far from being ſo defec-
tive that this bias towards variety may not be
gratified with books that tend at leaſt to pleaſe
the imagination, and not hurt the heart; for
though mere pleaſure be in ſome degree un-
worthy of our nature, yet the reading of ſuch
books as entertain us only, and are not intended to ſeduce the mind, is infinitely preferable to
thoſe peſtilential works, that though they may
indeed have charms to flatter a falſe taſte, yet
grievouſly miſlead the judgment, and corrupt
the morals of their reader. But we ſay, dear
children, that a library might be provided you,
nor that a ſmall one, of ſuch books as would
conduce to make you every day much better for
peruſing them, while they amuſed your fancy,
and agreeably employed your thoughts. Such
are, for inſtance, the Spectators, and thoſe other
periodical productions, that were publiſhed
nearly at the time when they appeared. Such
likewiſe are thoſe three great monuments of

found

found inftruction and fine writing: PAMELA,
CLARISSA, and the all accomplifhed GRAN-
DISON. Such too is that vaftfield of information,
or diffufive view of ait and the Almighty's
whole creation, in feven volumes if not more,
tranflated from a foreign language, and entitled
by its Editor, A View of Nature. Such are all the
admirable writings of a modein female, whofe
theatrical, but moral pieces, will remain on re-
coid as an honor to the country that produced
her, while a genius fertile for invention, and the
beauties of a chafte though ornamental ftyle,
have charms to pleafe the imagination. Her
dramatic pieces in particular, though fome objection may perhaps be made to fuch a channel
of inftruction, and what channel will defy all
cenfure? have this great advantage, that their very title page profefling to amufe, her little readers are deluded, as it were, into a wifh of reading, and if fuch a word may be allowed us,
cheated into virtue and improvement. Such
too,—but the lift of books that might be pitched
on at a minute's warning, to make up a large
collection of inftructive reading, would be end-
lefs: while, believe us, fuch as for example
fake one writer's, fince we have not read fuch
books ourfelf, and therefore are but little quali-

fied to furnish forth a catalogue for such as
might defire to be provided with thofe books,
which go the neareft way to work in ruining a
child's good principles ; fuch books, we fay, as
for example, of one writer, namely, Fielding,
who has ftrained his wit to make the ways of
guilty pleafure more inviting than they are
already to a vitiated tafte ; fuch books, we fay
once more, fo far from being put into the hands
of children, fhould be execrated by all thinking
people.

But, dear children, if your choice of books
fhould fall on thofe which most of all relate
to God, it follows, that provided there be
fuch a book as one, which wholly, or in every
page, has fuch relation ; *that*, we do not fay,
entirely, but much more than any other, fhould
employ your time. It is not neceffary we
fhould tell you there is fuch a book, videlicet, the Bible, which fhould therefore occupy
the greater part of your attention : on this
book, St. Paul pronounces an eulogium, as
the text informs you, when in one of thofe
epiftles he addreffed to his beloved Timothy,
he fays: *from a child thou haft known the holy
fcriptures, which are able to make thee wife unto
falvation, through faith which is in Chrift Jefus.*

To

To this commendation of the word of God,
dear children, we add nothing of ourfelf. Should
we employ much argument to prove the future
benefit refulting from the ftudy of this book?
It is defigned for your inftruction in the way of
righteoufnefs, which way, if you purfue it,
will conduct to God, while many of thofe
books which multitudes are fond of reading,
ferve the purpofe only of converting human beings into reprobates, before that time is come
when the affection of beholders gazing on the
beauty of their childhood, ceafes in the ftyle of
love and kindnefs to denominate them little angels.   And not only is this book, we mean the
Bible, preferable to all others for the future
benefit it will procure you; but that prefent
pleafure which may flow from its perufal, you
fhould look on as another ftrong inducement to
confider it the friend of your beft hours, the
partner of your heart, and the companion of
your youth: nay more; if at the prefent feafon of your life, you could experience the diftreffes of a bofom overwhelmed with forrow,
in that cafe, you fhould confider it a certain refuge from that forrow.   Do you love to weep
at the relation of a piteous tale?   Weep then
at the idea of God's friend, as he is called, we

mean

mean the faithful Abraham, when commanded
by the Almighty, as a trial of his faith, to facrifice his fon, the only one he had been bleffed
with, he is afked by this devoted fon while they
were going forward towards the place where
the fad ceremony was to be accomplifhed,
where the lamb was he defigned to facrifice?
and is thus anfwered. oh my fon ! God will provide himfelf with fuch a lamb.   Poor child, he
might have faid, at what a price does not thy father prove his faith and duty! dear, dear Ifaac,
thou fhalt be an angel in the courts of God, and
I fhall follow thee, though now like an unnatural
father, in the eyes of men, I lift my hand
againft thee, and pour out thy unoffending
blood. Weep on perufing the fad hiftory
of Jacob, when defrauded by his brother Efau
of a father's blefling, he enquires in fuch pathe-
tic language if that father has one fingle bleffing only he can give away?   Dear father, are
the words of Jacob, haft thou but one blefling
to beftow? blefs me, even me, my father , me
of whom you are fo fond. Weep when you
fee king David at the threfhing floor of Or-
nan, praying for his people, and imploring God
to turn on him the fury of his indignation. Is
it not, fays he, my fin, oh God, though oughteft

to

to punish? Smite it then in me. I have, alas!
deferved thy anger! but these unoffending lambs,
my fubjects, that at every hazard of my life I
fhould protect, what have they done? Thy
juftice be on me then, oh Lord God, and fpare
my people. Weep when you behold, in the
Apocrypha, a mother and feven children brave
the fury of Antiochus Dear children, how you
came into the world, fays this afflicted mother,
I can no how tell: but this I know is true;
that I could ever give you life and breath, or
afcertain by what ftrange means they were com-
municated to your frame. Weep when you view
Chrift Jefus fuffer on the crofs, but carelefs of
himfelf, employ his laft remaining moments in
the act of recommending to the well beloved
John, a mother he had always loved. Behold
thy mother, were his dying words. We might
go further, dear difciples, but we truft by this
time we have faid enough to fhow you, that of
books, the Bible fhould, in preference, occupy
your thoughts, and next thereto, fuch books as
have a reference to God, with which we clofe
our exhortation. Turn, dear children, to the
fecond book of Efdras, the eighth chapter, and
in that part you will fee how great a worth the
Jews annexed by their demeanour to this word

G 3

of

of God, when once again redeemed from
their captivity, they were convinced they
had before defpifed it. Opening, in the prefence of a multitude, God's word, this Efdras
read it from the morning till noon day, and all
the people wept in fuch a manner that the Le-
vites were obliged to go from rank to rank, that
they might comfort the affliction of the whole
affembly.   They remembered their iniquity,
and the Almighty's mercy; fwearing folemnly
they would in future really revere the word of
God.   Revere it therefore you, dear children,
that have never fcorned it.   Grant, oh God,
that as thy fervant Mofes, in his fong, addreffed
both earth and heaven in the fecond chapter of
his book of Deuteronomy, our doctrine may
come down into the hearts of thofe to whom we
preach, like rain upon the tender herb and
fhowers upon the grafs, that by the frequent
reading of thy word, they may acquire a knowledge of thy will, and gain that immortality it
was intended to procure thy children.   Grant
them fuch a blefling, for the fake of Jefus-
Chrift, &c.

THE.

THE HYMN,

FROM DR. WATTS.

IN many a work, by man compos'd,
   With profit I can look:
But perfect wifdom, power, and grace,
   Shine brightly in God's book.

There, are my choiceft treafures plac'd;
   There, my beft comfort lies,
There, my defires are fatisfied;
   And thence, my hopes arife.

There, I am told, Chrift fuffered death,
   To fave my foul from Hell:
Not all the books on earth befide
   Such heavenly wonders tell.

Then let me love my Bible, Lord,
   And therein take delight:
By day perufe thofe wonders o'er,
   And meditate by night.

G 4   SERMON

SERMON XXVI.

ON SLOTH.

MATTHEW xx. v. 6.

Why stand ye here all the day idle?

YOU know, as well as we do, little friends, how great a solace, that is confolation, you experience, when, as frequently it happens even to the child that has the beft of difpofitions, after having done a fault, or having left undone fome act of duty, you can any way excufe yourfelves. In that cafe, half your error, if not all, is done away, and they who are appointed to watch over you, and who, unlefs they act like brutes, no more delight to punifh you, than thofe to whom you are indebted for the gift of life and being, heartily rejoice to think they can perform their duty, and refrain from the infliction of that chaftifement they feared you merited for where is to be found that child who does not fome times ftand in need of being brought to an idea of its duty, by

a feem-a feeming harfhnefs in the teacher, governor, or parent, but which feeming harfhnefs is intrinfic, that is, real love? For even in God, his punifhments betoken his affection. Witnefs what St. Paul fays· *Whom the Lord loveth, he chafteneth, and fcourgeth every fon that is brought unto him.*

This excufe the people had, to whom the queftion in our text was put. The gofpel fays, " a certain perfon who poffeffed a vineyard, and " to whom, our Saviour tells us, God may be " compared, went out at different periods of " the day, (firft, early in the morning, then " at nine, twelve, three; and, laft of all, fo " late as five o'clock, which was no earlier " than a fingle hour before a working day was " ended,) hiring fervants every time. To thofe " he hired at five he faid, *why ftand ye idle here* " *all day?* and they replied, (their anfwer be- " ing the excufe we hinted at, and which muft " certainly be thought a very proper one) be- " caufe they had not been engaged or hired."

We do not here purfue the parable, becaufe, what it concludes with, may come in with more propriety when we have got a little further in our exhortation. We ftop fhort with their excufe, and freely, though affectionately,

G 5

little

little friends, inform you, that provided any one of you ſhould give occaſion, by your conduct in this place, or any other where you may be placed for education, to be aſked, *why you ſtand idle all day long?* or why, for want of due conſideration, you neglect the means afforded you of gaining knowledge or improvement, you will never have it in your power to plead the ſame excuſe, becauſe your daily work is ſet, becauſe you have your taſk before you, and becauſe your parents do not *wiſh* alone, but *charge* you to be diligent in ſtudy; anxious, as they are, that when you come to years of reaſon and reflection, you may every one appear among mankind with credit and repute. Since, then, you are without excuſe for indolence or ſloth, it will become you to avoid the charge, by diligently giving your attention to thoſe ſtudies which your parents pay to have you taught.

But, poſſibly, it may not be ſufficient to inform you of the duty you are under to be diligent in ſtudy! We muſt let you know the miſerable conſequences ſloth too often ends in; for thoſe miſerable conſequences, you will ſay, have never ſtruck you. True; you are not yet come forth into the walks of public life; and
they

they who do not own a providence that orders all things for the beft, might fay, it was not wifely ordered that young people, whofe profperity in life depends upon a prudent ufe of time while they are children, have not the advantage of experience to deter them from that floth which is the caufe why, generally fpeaking, they who pafs away their youth therein, incur diftrefsful fituations, when they reach the time of their maturity. Let us not murmur at the difpenfations of God's providence, however; for God's providence is more attentive to us than we merit it fhould be. Poor children! what would you do, in particular, if this were not a truth. When you were hanging on the breaft, it was the providence of the Almighty that protected you. In all the ailments childhood is expofed to feel, it was the providence of the Almighty that preferved your life; and, through the providence of the Almighty, *have you conftantly been holden up*, as David mentions, *ever fince your birth. Be then your praife at all times of it.* nor let him, we mean your preacher, who at prefent, in the ardour of his love, might poffibly be tempted to efpoufe your caufe too warmly, think of murmuring againft providence that has denied your childhood all the know-

G 6   ledge

ledge flowing from experience , but, poffeffing
fuch an ardent love, let him evince it by def-
cribing, from his own expeiience, the diftreffes
generally undeigone by multitudes who incon-
fiderately throw away the precious feafon of
their life, when youth fhould *fow* with diligence, that it may *reap* with gladnefs.   Some
of this great number have been only foolifh;
but their fortune has been fuch, that worfe
could not have happened to the guilty.   Like
the prodigal, they have been forced in anguifh
to cry out : " How many hired fervants in my
" father's houfe have bread enough, and more
" than they can want, while I am perifhing
" with hunger !" What more lamentable ex-
clamation, with refpect to earthly things, can
guilt be under the neceffity of making?

Hear what follows then —*A flothful man,*
fays Solomon, *hideth his hand in his bofom, and
will not fo much as bring it to his mouth again.*
Now this is a defcription, little ones, that
fhould for ever put you on your guard againft
becoming fuch a character as Solomon is fpeaking for , fo figure to yourfelves the winning
attitudes and elegant activity of children , they
are always wifh'ng to change place , they live,
as one would think, to be in conftant motion ;

and

and their playfulnefs is but another name for
exercife. That fpoit which makes the countenance fo cheeiful, renders the heart too as
glad. Inftead of which, the flothful perfon
buiies, that is hides, *his hand within his bofom.*
Would a figure, painted in this attitude, have
any beauty? But the worft is yet to come: for,
as the verfe goes on, *he will not bring it to his
mouth*; that is, he will not put himfelf into the
leaft degree of motion, were it barely to procure himfelf a maintenance. It follows then,
that floth ingenders poverty. This is the flight-
eft inconvenience that befalls it. The forlorn
condition of fo many round about our dwellings
proves no lefs.

Poor victims to the indolence of thofe who
fhould have fhown themfelves your parents, as
too many innocents that lead a life of wretchednefs in every quarter of the land muft be accounted, your unhappy fortune is a dreadful
proof that God, according to his menace, really
does vifit the iniquity of parents in their children, you have found, by miferable demon-
ftration, that your parents lived, not only ufe-
lefs in the world, but hurtful to you. Nature
fhould have pleaded for you in their hearts, and
faid, that when you afked them for a bit of
bread,

bread, they fhould not, on the other hand, have offered you a ftone; of which the worft that can be faid is, that it will not be of ufe to life: but, by their ruinous behaviour, they have held you out a ferpent that has hurt your life. Their floth, which, in its progrefs, has attained to the extremity of guilt, has left you, being females, folitary and abandoned in the world, fince educated without principles, you live the fhame and fcorn of your own fex. And you too, being males and heirs of equal mifery, have received a name for no one pur-pofe but to curfe the hour that gave you being, your unhappinefs, poor fufferers, firft ftruck root when your infatuated parents firft refigned themfelves to floth.

For how fhould fuch a vice have any other iffue, when we recollect that induftry was meant for man, and *that* too, when his dwelling was undoubtedly the faireft place in nature? You, good little ones, that read the Bible, know it was a garden: *God*, fays Mofes, *took the man that he had formed, and placed him in the garden;* (for, in Englifh, paradife means garden) the garden, we repeat, of Eden, *purpofely to drefs and keep it.* Induftry is therefore fuited to man's nature. It was not enjoined, or ordered him,

by

By way of punifhment; for, during the whole week preceeding this commandment laid on man to be induftrious, God had been employed in fafhioning the world wherein we live, the fun, and every ftar we fee above us, with the vaft profufion of trees, flowers, and other plants that fo enchant or pleafe our fight and other fenfes, with the multitude of creatures in whofe noftrils is the breath of life, and with whatever elfe has been created, all for the en‑joyment, ufe, and benefit of Adam's numerous pofterity; with which befides, the Almighty is defcribed as greatly pleafed himfelf, when he pronounced his whole creation very good. The induftry of man is therefore pleafing in the fight of God; and God defigned he fhould at all times be induftrious. Be induftrious, therefore, little children; to be flothful, is departing from the rule of nature, and the love of God. You are, methinks, fo many rifing *Adams*; and, as Adam was, are placed in a delightful garden, where fpring up unnumbered trees of knowledge, but whofe fruit you need not be afraid of plucking; in which point of view you are much better off than Adam, fince the tree of knowledge, planted in the midft of Eden, he was ordered not to tafte of, while

the

the order you receive is diametrically the reverse. This fruit, which you are charged to pluck, is the reward of induftry, and therefore, when we bid you be induftrious, it is only bidding you in other words be happy.

And be certain, this reward will come: for God, although he may be generous to profufion with refpect to fome, is notwithftanding juft to all · his lavifh bounty to a favourite will not let him overlook whatever the mere fervant may exert himfelf to do. The mafter of the vine-yard, as Chrift Jefus in the parable informs us, paid to thofe who had been labouring only for an hour, one penny, thofe who had been toiling the whole day expected he would give them more: but they received one penny. Now what reafon had the laft to murmur? he had ftipula-ted, that is bargained, with them for a penny; and a penny they received. This penny was enough, for, doubtlefs, it was cuftomary at that period to pay thofe that did day-labour, fuch a fum of money, and no greater. They received their due reward, then fellow workmen's pay, comparatively fpeaking greater, did not make them poor.

In this, dear little friends, learn refignation to God's will, and if in future, after having

laboured

laboured in the work of ftudy with inceffant application, and not only that, but after having
entered on that work as foon as you could take
a book in hand,—if after this, we fay, you
fhould obferve that others who have poffibly
beftowed lefs application on their ftudy, and
begun it at a later hour of life, are equally or
more advanced when men or women than yourfelves in thofe refpective fituations they have
gained by merit, be you notwithftanding happy
in your own allotment. No one fhould expect
a greater recompence than he deferves. You
have done every thing you could to merit more,
or like the vineyard-men have laboured the
whole day, and notwithftanding others, who
have worked no longer than an hour, have been
more bountifully paid, or got at leaft as much, yet
ftill remember you have had your wages. God
may do as he thinks proper with his own, and
you, that have enough, ought not to entertain
an evil eye or difcontented fpirit for no other
reafon than becaufe the eye or fpirit of your
God is good. To others, he has fhown himfelf profufely kind, to you he has not been
unkind. Make then the moft of what you have
received. it is God's gift, and if difcreetly huf-
banded, will be enough.

From

From what has been advanced, are you convinced that floth is what you ought to fhun,
provided you would gain a comfortable fituation in the world? But you may carry your
ideas farther, and be equally convinced that
floth fhould be avoided as a hindrance to that
much more comfortable fituation which awaits
you in the world to come, for as experience
tells us, all the virtues hang together, fo do all
the vices likewife : but we rather chufe to fix
your contemplation on the earthly recompence
of induftry, that you may be enamoured of it,
and fhun floth. The heavenly recompence
may, with much more propriety, become the
object of your contemplation at a future time.
We fay then, in one word, the earthly recompence of induftry is this,—that by it, you will
gain in youth the forecaft of old age, and, as
by induftry you will avoid temptations to irregular and vicious courfes, you will have, in age,
the undiminifhed faculties of youth. Your
days, as David calls them, *will be full*, and, if
you do not lofe the fpring-tide of your life in
pleafure and forgetfulnefs, you will be faved
from the calamitous neceffity of drawing out
the winter of your life in weaknefs and difeafe.

To

To you that are of fofter frame, let us addrefs a word or two before we finifh. Your condition in the world is fomewhat hard; and this we fay, by no means to deject or fadden you, but give fit reafons why you fhould apply yourfelves to this great work of ftudy. When you come into the world, you will experience how tyrannical is fafhion. Who are thofe that do whatever they are able to keep up that fafhion? Thofe, dear little friends, though it appear a contradiction, over whom this fafhion moftly plays the tyrant. Thofe, who having in their youth gone through a modifh education, have no ferious bufinefs or emplyment when they launch into the world, thofe who confume in fleep the better feafon of the day; who when they rife, fit down to that great work, the adornment of their perfon; thofe who are difguifed, or as they fay embellifhed, by thofe colours nature never gave them; thofe who when thy vifit, do fo to receive the homage of their friends for fome new garment they have juft before put on, and fpend the remnant of the day, till after midnight, at the theatre; or being much more culpable, perhaps fit down to play. If occupations of this fort can be called induftry, what then is floth? Thefe occupati-

ons

ons ruin families, and they muft be the occu
pations of all thofe that have no ufeful art, or
ceitainly, they would not fly to fuch irrational
expedients for the fake of diffipating time. And
would you, little ones, by imitating them in
childhood, be reduced to imitate them when
grown up. A wife, when frugal of hei time, is
often made a victim to her hufband's diffipation. what fad foitune then muft not attend a
diffipated wife? May you, dear little hcarei-,
never know fo fad a forune.

And may God, in his abundant mercy, fave
you every one from that defpair and ruin, indolence biings with it, fave you, on a future day
from the neceflity of chuling your amufemeuts,
by infpiring you with grace to know what
greater labour that neceffity is conftantly attended with, than any other toil May he inftiuct
you, that by application now to ftudy, fo that
when aiirived at years of reafon, you may pio-
perly difcharge the duties of your ftate, you will
be happy ; while by inattention now, you may
in future come to want May his good fpirit
dwell within you, may this habitation be your
ark, your fhelter, and, like Noah's dove, may
you at no time wifh to quit it, till impioved by
good inftructions, you go forth, affured of find-

ing

ing fafety in the company of thofe you mix
with. Be it fo through Jefus Chrift, &c.

THE HYMN.

OH God, who haft our bodies form'd
 Thus comely to the eye,
And wouldft not that the mind within
 Uncultivate fhould lie.

Give us, in thefe our early years,
 This one great thing to know:
That the mind's comlinefs alone
 From learning's fource fhould flow.

Then fhall we 'fcape that dangerous rock
 On which fo many run,
Sloth, whofe falfe charms whoever love,
 Too often are undone.

Let thofe among us who are rich
 Look round about, and fee
How often is brought down to want
 The man of high degree.

So,

So, while we ftudioufly attain
    The knowledge taught us here,
Each in his feveral ftate of life
    Shall, as he fhould, appear.

With dignity the rich ; and they
    Who muft fome calling chufe,
Taught, for the honeft means of life,
    Their feveral arts to ufe.

SERMON

SERMON XXVII.

ON GOOD AND BAD COMPANY.

I CORINTHIANS XV. V. 33.

Evil communications corrupt good manners.

HOW different, dear little ones, from such communications as corrupt good manners, are not thofe your preacher often has enjoyed, and ftill continues to enjoy, with fome among you! Neither was nor is there any evil to corrupt on one hand, and of courfe upon the other, no good manners were or are corrupted. This defcription is not half enough. There was and is, on one hand, innocence of manners; and of courfe, upon the other, thofe good manners he brought with him to enjoy the fweets of fo unblamable an intercourfe were then, and ftill are, rendered better. Every intercourfe partaken of with fuch endearing company, has been a feaft, delightful while it lafted; and the recollection of it, on the morrow was delightful alfo: they ftill yield the fatisfaction providence intended ed fhould proceed from fuch communications. They were fiift of all the occupation of his youth, his more advanced, yet not at prefent withering time of life purfues fo fweet an occupation ftill, and the remembrance of the formei, heightens the enjoyment of this laft.

From the above preamble, you will fee, dear children, what communications this difcourfe is likely to bring forward, as productive, on one fide at leaft, of joy and fatisfaction, mingled with no guile ; or rather, of fuch joy and fatisfaction, as are recommendable for the morality if not the virtue in them. Yes, foi to addrefs this part of our difcourfe to you that have already paffed the noon-tide of your days, and every moment of your lives are finding how much vanity there is in all thofe entertainments you were once fo fond of, but who more particularly have expeiienced the fallacious joys of thefe communications you have had with what aie called, and what you thought fo, namely, the choice fpirits of the age, of whofe fociety, at prefent, nothing but the guilt or naufea of it is remembered, come you over to the preacher's party, and as he does, foim communications with fuch company as will not only never render moie corrupt thofe vicious manners you have previ-

oufly

ously contracted in the company you mixed
with, but even render pure what was before
corrupted. Come with us to the society of such
as will not only be productive of your reforma-
tion, but improvement likewise.

And you little ones, give heed to thofe ob-
ftructions which the affection of your preacher
is addreffing to you.   Cultivate a friendfhip, or
connection, not alone with fuch as are in point
of age upon a level with you, and have feen no
more of this great world than you have, but
with thofe of longer ftanding, whofe experience
of it, is much greater than yours poffibly can be.
The advantages of fuch a friendfhip or connection will not all be on one fide.   You will indeed, not only charm as many as you mix with
of this laft defcription, and prefeive their morals uncorrupted, or make pure what was before
corrupted, but on their fide, they muft unavoidably improve and even pleafe *you.*   Yes; pleafe
you, we repeat; for pleafure you will find in-
volved in the improvement.   Nor are we to
wonder, in the leaft, that pleafure fhould refult from intercourfes of this nature, for in this
as well as other matters, is the obfervation of a
poet verified, that what he calls the *difcords* of
all nature, are intended to keep up the *concord* of

all nature ; which is just the same as saying, if
the obfervation be applied to this one fubject we
are now employed on, that the foftnefs and the
innocence which are at prefent fo inherent to
you, fhall correct the harfhnefs and propenfity (at leaft) to guilt of thofe whofe friendfhip
you are recommended to purfue or cultivate ;
while, on the other hand, their knowledge and
experience fhall affift your want of knowledge,
and the inexperience naturally cleaving to your
years

Whatever has been hitherto advanced, has
gone upon a fuppofition that both parties had
had no end in view to prejudice each other;
for, dear children, how can you be looked upon
as capable of entertaining fuch a wicked view?
and what defign can others, more advanced in
life, have any intereft to form againft the peace
and innocence of perfons young as you ?   The
text then has not been as yet made applicable,
but the time will very fhortly come, and is, as
one may call it, with refpect to fome at leaft
among you, even at the door, when you will
ferioufly begin to form connections.   Such
then we addrefs with what is to fucceed, nor
will the reft beneath them in refpect to age, be
prejudiced or injured by our argument.   We
there-

therefore fay to thofe whom more particularly now we have in view, remember, little friends, that as the text expreffes it, *bad company, or bad communications, vitiate or corrupt good manners.* Let this obfervation be at all times in your memory, when, amid the multitude furrounding you, and fome of them defigning very likely to corrupt your morals, you would feek companions, and make bofom friends of fuch, when you have found them.

It is juft the fame in matters of the moral, as in thofe, dear children, of the natural world; for dangers hem you in on every fide, and whether you are looked upon as creatures merely breathing, or as pufhing their exiftence to a future ftate of being, in both cafes, you have equal reafon for alarm, on one hand, to effect the fafety of your frame, and on the other, of your foul. for, would you think it? thofe who are much converfant in calculations of mortality, affure us that in towns, no parent has great reafon to expect his child will live beyond the age of feventeen years: and if a fingle child furvives that age, fixteen muft fomewhere or another die before it. Miferable parents! do you place your hopes of happinefs on rearing to maturity a family? and taking parents all together, fhall

you

you fee your children drop before the time of
feventeen years is paft? Oh the flight bafis
upon which all human expectations or defires
are founded, when this expectation or defire of
what the Pfalmift calls a heritage, that fhall
fucceed to be the prop and pillar of your age,
as well as live to take poffeffion of your ho-
nors, and not only that, but be the means of
propagating both your name and memory in
the world,—when, we repeat, this expectation
or defire, which is the greateft man can poffibly indulge in, is fo quickly overthrown! but
this is not the worft · we mean this fituation of
affairs as far as they regard the natural world,
fince in the moral world too, there is equal
reafon why we fhould live conftantly in fear of
danger that may happen to the fouls of rifing
individuals, juft as in the former cafe, there
was refpecting danger happening to their perfons, for how numerous are not the incentives
to affociate with bad company, and thefe, the
Apoftle tells us, cannot but corrupt good manners. Wonderful muft it indeed be looked
upon, that any can efcape the dangers, which in
this refpect continually threaten ! We, for our
part, know of no defence againft them, but God s
grace. Pray, therefore, in the firft place, that

your

your choice of such companions as shall not corrupt you, may be prudently directed. All the instruction men could give you in a thousand exhortations, would not have a thousandth part of its effect.

The danger of associating with bad company is to be feared the more, because, like every other sin, when we are once accustomed to it, we discern how difficult it is to throw off such communications as corrupt good manners: but though difficult, still is it practicable, or by great exertions, to be done. and will not even the disorder be a great inducement with you to work out its cure? for other maladies will frequently supply those medicines that at last remove them.—thus the sin of luxury, or lavish living, when the prodigal no longer has it in his power to waste, is cured. Think *you* then if at any time you shall have got within the influence of those communications that corrupt good manners,—think, we say, that the apparent danger you are every hour exposed to, far from being a discouragement, should animate you to determine on abjuring those communications Some, we know, have thought a sort of honorable tie was on them not to shun that company they have already chosen, but what

honor-

honorable tie can such bad company suggest? They who do all they can to vitiate your good morals? Read, dear children, in God's word what rule such people as the Apostle had in view, when he was writing his epistle to the men of Corinth, and of which, our text, we need not tell you, is a part.—Read in God's word, we say, what rule such people have to regulate their conduct. While you court their company, and consequently are as wicked as themselves, they will assist you with their counsels, but when once you come into such situations as suggest amendment, and provided in such situations you have need of their assistance, will they then cleave to you? When the unnatural Absalom made insurrection in the city of Jerusalem, and sought by favour of the people to dethrone his father, oh then, little ones, he found himself by no means in a want of friends: but when abandoned by his party, after the defeat he met with, and then needing their assistance, they forsook him, and even Joab, who had been his friend while his prosperity continued, was no sooner told of his suspension to the branches of a tree that caught him up while he was passing under it, than with a savage fury in his heart, he posted to the spot

and

and thruſt him through the body. This is one ſad inſtance, not of the corruption of good morals only, which mankind are liable to undergo from bad communications, though indeed, ſince that corruption is the ruin of their ſouls, one would imagine it enough, but likewiſe of their ruin in this world, the forfeiture of all their expectations, and their premature deceaſe, that is to ſay their death, before the time is come by nature. Take another inſtance. Would the prodigal, whoſe melancholy fate we have ſo frequently adduced for your inſtruction, and with great propriety, ſince Jeſus Chriſt ſuppoſed the caſe of ſuch a youth as what would furniſh an important leſſon, and whatever he ſuppoſed for ſuch a purpoſe, is well worthy man's attention every moment of his life, while he has any being—would the prodigal, we ſay, have been deſerted in his adverſe fortune, if the company he had before hand kept were not of ſuch a caſt as the Apoſtle hints at? Miſerable youth!—You fed them, at your table, with the choiceſt viands; and, in your adverſity, had not that food the very ſwine were fed with Woe is me! we think we hear you ſaying, my companions have occaſioned me the loſs of every thing;

the

the lofs of my late fubftance, of my conftitution, of my health, and of my father!—Oh, if they had not deferted me before-hand, with what eafe would I not now have fled from them! Thrice happy, had I only done as much before they joined together to deprive me of my patrimony, and reduce me to want bread. If this be not fufficient, take one more example. for would David, but for bad companions and their wicked counfels, have been fo supported, when he undertook the murder of Uriah, being fet on fire to gain poffeffion of Bathfheba's charms? but being not long after that, well nigh abandoned, when the treafon of his well-beloved Abfalom broke forth, and, with a few of his domeftic fervants, he was forced to quit the city of Jerufalem, leaft he fhould fall a facrifice, and was, as it appears, fo very heartleis, that the ark of God, which thofe attend-ing on his flight bore with them for their mafter's fafety, would not, he imagined, fave him from the malice of his enemies? a fuppofition evident from what he faid, as follows· *Carry back the ark of God into the city, if I fhould find favour in his fight, then will he bring me back again, and grant me to behold both that, and with it too, his holy habitation. But provided he*

fhould

*should say I have no pleasure in thee; here I am;
let him do every thing his providence thinks proper.*
Thefe are three examples of the dangerous confequences flowing from bad company; and
which we meant to fhow you. Take advantage of them, and, inftructed by the leffon
they contain, be wife, and form no bad connections; or, provided you fhould have already
formed them, do your utmoft to divide the
bands that hold you to them, and be free in
future.

We were minded with this obfervation to
conclude; but there is one thing more, of
which we would forewarn you; though the
caution we fhall give hereafter, in another
drefs of language, namely: that all fellowfhip
with thofe that are unequal to you, be they
your fuperiors or inferiors, fhould be ftudioufly
avoided. And if matters in reality are fo, how
much the more, dear children, is it not your
duty to avoid all commerce and connection
with as many as appear in point of virtue your
unequals? By this inequality of virtue, have a
multitude of otherwife well-meaning youths, both
male and female, been undone. Avoid, then,
their unhappy fortune, and depend upon yourfelves, with the Almighty, for that favourable

profpect

profpect you may form of your affairs in this
world, no lefs fo than for that final happinefs
you wifh to have in future. Oh almighty
father of the world, whofe providence is the
fupport of every creature thou haft made, while
man is thy diftinguifhed care, and children
more particularly hang upon thee for protection—to thefe children we requeft thou wouldft
extend thy fatherly affection, and at prefent
being planted, as they are, in Eden, let them
ftill continue in that ftate of innocence which,
in reality, fo pure a habitation needs, and
that this innocence may not be blighted in its
bloffom, but bring forth abundant fruit hereafter, guard them, we befeech thee, from the
multiplied feductions of the world, and from
the ruin of bad company that fhall convert the
Eden they now live in, and in which they are
fo happy, into an unjoyous wildernefs, where
nothing fhall be found to grow for their fub-
fiftence. Always let them have in view the
fate of our firft parents after they were difpof-
feffed of Eden, and infpire them with an underftanding to compare their former with their
latter fituation; the idea upon one hand of thy
prefence, and thofe angry cherubims upon the
other, that were placed to keep the garden, and
prevent

prevent them from returning. So too let them argue with themfelves, and not for fome few pleafures they may fancy in bad company, permit their morals to become corrupt, and fo exchange the enjoyments of their prefent happy fituation, having every thing provided to their hand for the diftreffes of another fituation, which not only fhall fubject them to the bitter confequences of thy judgment in a future world, but likewife to a want of every thing in this. Hear us, we pray thee, for the fake of Jefus Chrift, &c.

THE HYMN.

GIVE me the grace, oh Lord, to chufe,
   For my companions here,
   Such as I need not fear
Will my good faith and love abufe.

Convinc'd, as I muft be, that none
   My friendfhip fhould partake,
   Who not for virtue's fake
A falfe friend's odious name will fhun.

H 6

And

And when, in confequence of thought,
  I've fix'd, give me a heart
  Not eafily to part
From them for any trivial fault.

My prayer I cannot well purfue ;—
  Give me thy grace alone,
  That always fhall make known
Whatever thou would'ft have me do.

SERMON

SERMON XXVIII.

ON THE JUSTICE AND MERCY OF GOD.

EXODUS XX. V. 5. 6.

I, the Lord, thy God, am a jealous God; visit-
ing the iniquity of the fathers upon the children
unto the third and fourth generation of them
that hate me; and showing mercy unto thou-
sands of them that love me, and keep my com-
mandments.

AND is it true then, you will very possibly
enquire, dear children, of your preacher,
that God visits, or, as lately we explained it,
punishes the wickedness of parents in their
children,—in their children, whose simplicity
or innocence we have so often mentioned is
entitled to the happiness of Heaven? How
can that punishment, and this simplicity or innocence, be suited to each other?

Yes,

Yes, dear children, it is true, that God *does* punifh frequently the wickednefs of parents in their children; and, what more perhaps may puzzle your conceptions to account for, in the children of thofe children, and even lower ftill: but though this threat of the Almighty may perplex your tender underftanding, be of comfort notwithftanding, for the object of this vifitation is not everlafting punifhment, but only temporary pains, and thofe too, nothing but the confequences which iniquity in this world always muft draw after it. God's fyftem of proceeding therefore is not to be wondered at, even if he were not God, whofe mercy is confpicuous in his juftice to mankind; but only placed above us, as a ruler. It is unavoidable but that the fin of every human being fhould be followed with innumerable inconveniences; not only to himfelf, but others round about him. and thofe inconveniences, dear children, are the punifhment with which God vifits the iniquity of fathers in their children. Sometimes, muft we own, the reafon of his conduct in fuch punifhment is not fo very clear, as in the cafe of David, and the child Bathfheba bore him, who, by reafon of its father's fin, was ftruck with death, for how can we conceive
that

that fuch a death fhould be the confequence alone, and nothing elfe, of that abominable fin the father had committed? but however unaccountable this circumftance may feem, ftill are we bound to have fuch thoughts of God, as not to think he can in any action be unjuft, and much lefs fo to innocent and unoffending little ones.

But if the haplefs fortune of this little one excite your pity, fmitten as he was, and feparated from the living, for his father's fin, what tears would you not fhed were this great world and all the fecrets of it, (fecrets as they muft be to your inexperienced minds) at once thrown open to your view? for David's little child endured the pain of dying only, which, comparatively fpeaking, is but momentary, and loft nothing; being fundered from a world, in which, with other human beings, he would certainly have fuffered greatly, to enjoy a place in paradife, without that toil which thofe whofe lives are lengthened out upon the earth, muft undergo to merit it. whereas, a multitude among us, fuffering equally with David's tender infant, for the fins of others, and in general too, of thofe they fpring from, undergo the pain of living

many

many years in such a state, that death perhaps
would be a medicine to relieve them.

Understand us properly, however, for in
many cases, they who suffer thus, have not the
sins of others to alledge in their excuse.   Those
sins indeed might very possibly have laid the
ground work of their wretchedness ; but they
continue wretched, or more wretched than they
would be otherwise, because they sin themselves.
It would be utterly impossible to put this argument in all the lights and situations it may
have.   We sum up therefore the whole matter
by observing, in the first place, that bad parents
have bad children, since in consequence of
that corrupt or vicious education they have had,
it is not probable they should be virtuous in
themselves they suffer therefore all the misery
their parents suffered.   And in this is seen the
equity of God, that is to say, his justice, who
makes parents, (as they ought to be) accountable for the prosperity or welfare of their children.   How incumbent therefore is it not on
parents, when the evil spirit possibly may set
them on committing such or such a crime, to
hesitate, and say: " if I give way on this oc-
" casion, I shall do a deed that probably will
" shed its mischiefs upon all my innocent de-
" scendants,

" fcendants, who for thirty, fixty, or a hundred
" years perhaps, will fuffer for the fhort lived
" pleafure that now tempts me." Parents, if
this argument does not affect you, where are
thofe compunctious feelings of the heart, by
nature, not to fay religion, commonly fuggefted?

In the next place, we obferve, dear children,
that good parents have good children, and then
circumftances are reverfed or altered. We
fhall not detain you by enlarging on thofe circumftances farther than by faying here, that
thefe good children in themfelves enjoy the
bleffings their good parents were rewarded with
before them. And in this, we may difcover
the benevolence of God, that is to fay his mercy, who encourages the parent to be virtuous,
from a certainty that the reward and comfort
of his virtues fhall defcend to thoufands fpring-
ing from him. Now, this equity of God, that
is to fay, his juftice, joined to this benevolence,
that is to fay his mercy, are the two grand
points on which, in this difcourfe, we meant to
give you fome fmall matter of inftruction.

You all wifh for life. It is fo fweet, you
cannot poffibly do otherwife Dear children,
may your wifh, which is fo natural, and which
God's

God's law does not prohibit, may your wish,
we fay, be gratified. May you in fafety pafs
the ftreights of childhood, and expatiate happy
on the plane of man or womanhood   You will
have other views then rife within your bofom
You will wifh for children.   May this wifh be
likewife gratified   May you have children.
May they every day grow up in ftature, and in
virtue, to rejoice you : but that this fame confequence more furely may take place, remember
what you are to hear at prefent, or remember
rather what God's law in fuch clear terms informs you of, that, as already we have faid, he
vifits the iniquity of fathers on their children.
When, by God's permiffion you are parents,
you will find that nothing can defcribe the feelings of a father or a mother's tendernefs, and
more particularly fo the laft. Let then the inftruction held you out at prefent, dwell particularly on your tender minds. Accuftom them
betimes to virtue, that whenever you have little
ones yourfelves, your fatherly or motherly affection may not feel one pang arifing in you,
from the dreadful probability that children
born to wretched parents, will themfelves be
wicked, and of courfe unhappy, for God's menaces muft always be fulfilled, if what thofe
me-

menaces were uttered to produce, does not take place, we mean a virtuous life in parents, founded on the thought that every vice they perpetrate will be feverely punifhed in the little ones born to them, in thofe little ones they are inftructed fo to love by nature.

Still, however, you may find it difficult to comprehend, that God does vifit, in reality, the fins of parents on their children, and the infant born to David being only one example, may not forcibly enough convince you. Liften, therefore, to a tale derived from real life; and having nothing but the probable, which will preclude your future doubt · for you, Eliza,—but we paufe, and afk ourfelf if it be proper to hold up a fuffering individual in this manner; and particularly having done fo once already? But what mifchief can enfue from thus exhibiting, by way of warning, an unhappy woman? We defign not to infult her in the hour of her calamity, if it have not, by this time, bowed her to the grave: nor do we know what detriment, to any individual, our proceeding will occafion   You then, we repeat, Eliza, are a dreadful proof that God, in his eternal juftice, vifits children for the perfonal tranfgreffion of their fathers.   Your's, alas! firft

fuffered

fuffered for *his* father, who prefering robbing
and fraud, to honefty and labour, was companion to a gang that made it their whole bufinefs to defraud the revenue, and could find
means, like others, to conciliate fuch a practice to his confcience, by the title pretext,
that private people are not injured by it, but
the land at large. This life of robbery and
fraud he followed many years, till government,
made privy to his malverfation, fent forth officers to feize upon his veffel, and take prifoner
every one on board her. With this veffel they
fell in, agreeably to information, an engage-
ment inftantly began, his crew was maftered,
and himfelf made prifoner. In the night that
followed, horrible to mention! he confpired,
together with the fharers of his wretched for-
tue, to commit a far worfe crime than that he
had been hitherto engaged in, rofe upon his
conquerors, and, impelled as much by vengeance as a wifh of freedom, murdered every one
on board the royal veffel, and regained poffeffion of his own. But what were he and his
affociates now to do? The deed of blood which
they had perpetrated was of fuch a nature, that
they could not hope to fhow themfelves in
England. He we fpeak of, with the reft,
                                        conccaled

concealed themfelves: his property was feized upon by government, or, as they fay, exchequered, while the wretched owner, feeing to what ftate he was reduced, deftroyed himfelf.

His fon, from whom you drew your life, Eliza, was not then grown up to man's eftate; and, having fuch a parent, we may naturally think, he had not been brought up, or educated, with much care. He was, in fact, a monfter of iniquity already, he had learned to fwear, loved gambling, and would even beat his mother, whofe fmall fortune, which had formerly been fettled on her, was not large enough to keep them both, and furnifh the unnatural fon with money for his pleafures By his cruel treatment fhe died very foon, quite broken hearted. He was now poffeffed of, what the lawyers call, her jointure. With the produce of it he came up to London, and gave thofe acquainted with him fome fmall hopes, when they were told he had procured himfelf a farm near town, and, in reality, we muft allow his conduct was, in fome fort, decent, if it had not been for his intolerable vice of fwearing, which encreafed upon him every day to fuch a great degree, that he could hardly fpeak two words together without thrufting in the name

of

of God, or Chrift, in junction with an execration, that is oath, between them.   Such a vice
was, of itself, fufficient to deftroy him, neither was it long before he took to liquor, and
foon afterwards, conceiving a prepofterous wifh
of marrying, as they fay, into a noble family,
for he had got acquainted with a needy female,
who was miftrefs of a title we muft own, but
not a fixpence to fupport her pride, he wed-
ded her.   This match, unfortunate Eliza,
which took place before you came into the
world,—and would to God it never had been
thought of, if that circumftance might have
availed to fave you from the pain of being in
the world,—this match, this fatal union, we
repeat, even had there been no other caufe of
ruin, would have overwhelmed him.   For a
year, or fo, about which period you were born
into a world of forrow, for a world of forrow
furely has it been to you, things went on toler
ably well between them, though, before that
time, your father had one morning been ar-
refted, even in his bed, for debts contracted
by his wife before they came together; and
thefe debts, which law compels a hufband to
difcharge, were all the miferable dower fhe
brought him, fave, as we have faid before, her

pride

pride and title. Love, however, or what people call by that foft name, was not extinguifh-
ed then between them, fo that fuch a matter of
humiliation or furprize, while it befel your father, did not caufe a rupture. But this rupture happened quickly after, for the time
that fhould have been devoted to the care and
culture of your little perfon, was confumed in
gaming, and, its fifter vice, (for they are generally fifters) drinking; which your mother,
never famous for fobriety, now gave a loofe to,
and indulged in. Swearing, in the interval,
and drunkennefs, grew daily on your father,
who beheld that partner—yes, that partner he
firft took to be his helpmate—die a victim to
the liquor fhe was fwallowing daily in fuch
great abundance. Debts were, in the interim,
increafing; and your father's conftitution,
though much ftronger than his partner's, funk
at laft beneath the preffure of his vices, which
increafed as he grew older. He furvived, fome
little time, a loathfome object of difeafe, and
died in agony, not having wherewithal to pay
his debts, much lefs then make provifion for
your maintenance, which was, alas! more
needful, as that fpecies of affection he poffeffed,
had never minded him to give you any education.

tion. He expired, in fhort, quite deftitute ;
not dropping like ripe fruit in autumn, but his
leaf fell off before the fummer was half gone :
and thus did the Almighty vifit, in his juftice,
the iniquity a father had committed in his
fon, yet were not the unnatural parent's vices
wholly the occafion of his wretched fon's fad
fortune? To the vicious education he had previoufly received, he added a propenfity to vice,
and therefore merited his punifhment.

But as for you, Eliza, what are we to fay?
That you were no lefs guilty, and that all the
miferies you fuffered were defervedly entailed
upon you! God has, in his juftice, punifhed
the iniquity committed by a father in his child,
and, as your melancholy cafe evinces, in his
grand-child alfo. May his rigorous arm ftop
here; or rather, if a namelefs progeny already
has defcended from you, may his mercy fpare
that progeny, for has not his feverity proceeded far enough? *On her*, may we, with David,
fay, *may all God's juftice be exhaufted* But,
alas! what have thofe lambs, defcended from
her, done? Oh God of mercy, as thou art,
if this unhappy victim to her own iniquity,
and that committed by her parents, be ftill living, vifit her with confolation, and remove for

ever the intolerable burthen of her mifery
and fin. Thy power can from the rock itfelf
draw water, and even caufe the flames to
comfort and refresh thy children in the furnace. Comfort and relieve, then, this afflicted object of thy wrath, for thou canft do fo ;
and then, ftill more gracious, let her be the
firft,—as probably fhe will be if thy mercy
vifit her diftrefs,—the firft of her unhappy family, in whofe behalf thy promife fhall be verified, of fhewing mercy unto thoufands in as
many as may love thee, and purfue the way of
thy commandments. Hear us for the fake of
Jefus Chrift, &c.

THE HYMN.

JUST are God's ways ; yet full withal
    Of mercy to mankind :
For finners, that deferve their fall,
    That fall are fure to find.

But for the juft, though fcorn and pride
    Faftidious tread them down,
Thy goodnefs fhall, oh Lord, provide
    In Heaven a glorious crown.

Recall not then the fins of yore,
　My anceſtors have done,
Or I ſhall periſh, Lord, before
　My years are well begun.

Nor let me ſin myſelf, leaſt they
　That to my name ſucceed,
Should of my ſins the forfeit pay,
　For ſuch, if I may plead.

SERMON

SERMON XXIX.

ON THE THIRD COMMANDMENT.

EXODUS XX. V. 7.

Thou shalt not take the name of the Lord thy God in vain; for the Lord will not hold him guiltless that taketh his name in vain.

DEAR little friend, Simplicius, why on such a subject as the present cannot you address our hearers, on the subject of this exhortation? but alas! you are departed, after having caused your parents, during the whole course of your short life on earth, no other lasting grief than what proceeded from the circumstance of having lost you. And that gentle spirit which, inspiring, as it did, the loveliest form that ever yet existed, or shall ever do so, was the joy and consolation of your parents, is now permanently happy in the company of angels and archangels. You, on this occasion, might inform those little ones we are addressing now,

of

of fin indeed committed at a very early period
of your life, in which the heart however had no
malice to account for, but of fubfequent repentance for that fin, in which the grace of God,
vouchfafed you at a period no lefs early, fhone
confpicuous. Situated like the little Samuel,
God thought fit to call you, and thofe parents his good pleafure had beftowed upon you,
were not lefs folicitous than Samuel's to make
known, that if God knocked once more, you
fhould reply: " fpeak Lord, for I thy fervant
" hear thee." And God certainly did fpeak;
or whence thofe edifying words, that when your
little body lay in anguifh, and was finally con-
vulfed upon a death bed,—whence, we fay,
thofe edifying words, than which, the lip of
age and wifdom could not furely have pronounced more edifying?—Whence, we fay once
more, thofe edifying words that while they pe-
netrated to the heart of your afflicted parents,
and entirely overwhelmed it for the moment,
made them in the fequel fo fuperlatively happy?
To this hour, they frequently talk of you, while
both wait, if we may fo exprefs ourfelf, God's
voice to render up their fpirit, and depart, if
fuch be his good will, together? " The dear
" child," they fay, " is gone before us; and
his

" his bleffed fpirit, when we die, fhall welcome
" us to that abode which, it might feem, we
" gave him life and being to partake of "
But we dwell too long on what concerns the
parents of the child we were fo fond of,
therefore, to be brief, his ftory is as follows .—

Sitting on his mother's knee one evening,
(it was *that*, as we remember of his birth day,
when ourfelf and others were invited by his parents to partake on the occafion of a little entertainment) : fitting on his mother's knee, we
fay, and having open on the table to amufe his
his little mind, a bible which his father had
juft bought him, ornamented with fine copper
plates, he was extremely bufy with them, and at
every cut he came to, would turn round, and
afk his mother what it meant. *Who pray is
this old man in bed*, particularly we remember
was his queftion, looking at the cut where
Ifaac bleffes Jacob, taking him for Efau : *the
old man feems blind; and this too, ftanding by
the bed, has hairy gloves on; what can all this
fignify?* The mother's anfwer needs not here
be mentioned. After this, proceeding in the
earneft work he was engaged in, and enquiring
what the fubject of each picture was, one we
remember, of the number, ftruck him more

than

than any of the others. *And what pray is this?*
said he   Be it fufficient to inform you, he
was looking at the RESURRECTION ; and in
confequence of many queftions, put on the occafion to his mother, which we need not here
repeat, he happened to be told that fwearing
was a fin, and that all fwearers would inevitably
go to hell

Some time, perhaps five minutes after this,
Simplicius wanted to go out   He went , but
no one of the company perceived him any way
affected.   Yet he was ; for being abfent longer
than was neceffary, his uneafy parents fent to
fetch him in ; when lo ! a cry was heard.   A
parent's hearing is much more upon the watch
than other people's.   They were inftantly
alarmed   They quitted the apaitment, and we
followed, running to the quarter whence the
noife proceeded , when behold ! we found the
little innocent Simplicius, in a fwoon, upon the
feat.   The parents' affiduities were all exeited
to reftore him. *My dear fellow,* were the mother s firft enquiries, when Simplicius was ref-
tored a little, and feemed capable of anfwering
her, *what ails you? tell me* " I fhall go to
" hell, mama," replied Simplicius, in a faulter-
ing kind of voice. *To hell; my child !* returned
                                    the

the mother? *God forbid!* " Yes yes, ma-
" ma, to hell, for would you think it, I have
" been this long time paft a fwearer," faid
Simplicius. *Been this long time paft a fwearer,*
my fweet little man, refumed his tender but afto-
nifhed mother; *do you fay fo really? this long time*
paft a fwearer! recollect yourfelf, dear child, if you
are able. You, a common fwearer! can you be fo?
why we never heard you fwear! " No, no, be-
" caufe I always fwear," replied Simplicius, to
myfelf. " That Samuel, lately turned away,
" fwore fo that I confidered it quite pretty to
" do juft the fame as he did; fo that now the
" devil will be fure to have me."

We break off in this part of our ftory. The
dear good Simplicius was confoled or comforted
by his indulgent parents, who affected with their
child's behaviour, and the thought that God of
his abundant grace fo early had addreffed his
little heart, returned him their unfeigned thanks;
and on the fpot, avowed that this, fo far from
being an affliction to them, was the happieft
birth day they had ever known fince firft their
dear Simplicius came into the world. Simplicius, after this, avoided fwearing as he would
have done a ferpent in the way; and promifed
to become a very virtuous youth. but God

I 4   thought

thought proper to remove him fhortly after.
A diforder fatal to fo many in the land, attack-
ed him: he funk under its feverity: he died:
but, to the joy and tranfport of his parents,
who had always been accuftomed to draw comfort from the providence of God in every circumftance befalling them, his death was fuch as
to confirm the affertion of the pfalmift, namely:
" In the mouth of babes and fucklings, God has
" willed that ftrength fhould be ordained, and
" from them praife proceed. ' His death, in
fhort, when time had taken off a little from
their forrow for his lofs, was matter of thankf-
giving to God's providence, for having thus
tranflated their beloved little one from earth to
an inheritance of happinefs, and ever fince
have they been anxious fo to frame their lives,
that they may go to him, though he, as they are
fenfible, will never come again to them.

From this affecting, but yet pleafing ftory,
learn dear little ones, to fhun the vice of fwearing, or, provided, as is not impofible, you
have unhappily adopted it in fecret, imitate
Simplicius in your forrow and repentance,
which can never come too late: much more
then will that forrow and repentance be accept-
ed, which is entered into at your early time of
life.

life. One fpecies of it, which is more than what we underftand by fwearing in the common acceptation of the term, as for example's fake, when human beings call on God to hurl d——n on their heads, and blaft,—but we proceed no farther: the defcription being of itfelf fo fhocking; therefore is it totally unneceffary we fhould put you on your guard againft this fpecies of the vice we preach upon, fince, being as it is, fo execrable, you will fcarce be guilty of a crime with which the vileft only, and the loweft of mankind, are to be charged. By fwearing, all we mean is the irreverent ufe of thofe two words, that is to fay, the name of God and Jefus, which on every flight occafion men, and fometimes women, introduce in their difcourfe.

The fum of our inftruction therefore on this fubject, needs not many words. Let not the names of God or Jefus ever iffue from your lips, excepting when you pray, or are engaged in very folemn converfation. By obferving this plain precept in your childhood, you will gain perfection with refpect to that command-ment which forbids your taking, as it fays, God's name in vain; and only by fuch means will you be able to refrain from violating, that is, breaking the commandment; for you know

I 5   the

the force of cuftom: practices, not only fuch
as yield no pleafure, but even fuch as in themfelves are highly painful, if in childhood you
affect them, will become habitual, and the difficulty, as perhaps fome here may know full well,
will *then* be to forego them. Shall we mention one?
that ungenteel, that vulgar action, which a multitude of children, we may fay, are fond of,
when they torture their own flefh, and eat away
their very fingers' ends ; for this they generally
do, and not disfigure only, or deform the nails,
which but for fuch a practice, would fo admira-
bly heighten and fet off the beauty of a well
fhaped hand.   You, therefore, that are guilty,
—for that term, we muft refort to, of this practice, or who note the guilt of it in others, afk
yourfelves if any thing, except the power of cuftom, and the difficulty of refraining from bad
habits, is the caufe why we obferve fo many
flunted,—the expreffion, we are now to add,
may very likely be accounted rather too un-
courtly, yet becaufe no wounds can poffibly affect our fenfe like foundnefs, and becaufe we
would do every thing we can to cure the rifing
generation of fo foul a practice, we muft ufe it,
therefore we renew the queftion,--what, except
the power of cuftom, and the difficulty of refraining

fraining from bad habits, is the caufe why we obferve fo many *ftunted ftinking* fingers' ends among us.

Give not then into a cuftom, in your youth, which is ridiculous as well as wicked. but remember what God fays to thofe who take his name in vain,—*I will not hold him guiltlefs that does fo.* And recollect too, that Chrift Jefus, in the prayer he taught us, has begun it with an article exprefsly to that purpofe. *Hallowed be thy name*. that is, account it holy. Holy it fhould be indeed; for in the troubles of this life, fays David, fpeaking in the fpirit, call upon me, and be certain I will hear thy prayer. The world is full of mifery, but oh God! thy name is fweet. The fame is to be faid of Chrift, for as the angel faid to Jofeph, *thou fhalt call him Jefus:* and why fo? *becaufe he is ordained to fave his people from their fins.* Now Chrift, and Jefus, are the fame, not fpelt alike indeed, or founding fo, but both relating to the Saviour. He then that fhall ufe the name of Chrift irreverently, is as culpable as he that ufes fo the name of Jefus God, and Chrift, or Jefus may be worthily employed, when we are in diftrefs, on urgent, that is, great occafions, and whenever we may need that aid,

I 6   which

which we have leave, nay which we are commanded, to implore through our Redeemer's name.
How then can we be juftified in uſing, upon
every trifling ſubject in diſcourſe, two names
that ſhould be only had recourſe to in our
wants? Think, little ones, that certainly a
time will come, though now your conſtitution
ſeems as if it were not to be ſhaken, when each
faculty you are poſſeſſed of will grow weaker
with your waſting frame: when, as Chriſt Jeſus
ſaid to Peter, though at preſent every day you
gird yourſelf, and go wherever you think fit,
another ſhall in future time, that is to ſay when
you are ancient, carry you where you would
not; ſoon after which, a death bed will conclude your life. Think, therefore, ſo that by a
good foundation, laid in childhood, you may
be prepared for ſuch a mournful time, when
you will naturally, as it were, pronounce the
name of God and Chriſt, as your laſt hope.
*Receive, oh God, my ſpirit, for the ſake of Jeſus
Chriſt*, will be your ſupplication. But what
hope will you derive from thoſe two names, if
in the courſe of your preceding life, you have
deſpiſed them? Nothing will enſure you the
divine aſſiſtance, which all thoſe who call on
God through Jeſus Chriſt are ſure they ſhall
receive,

receive, except the proper ufe of two fuch holy names, while you are young and healthful. Sanctify then, little ones, your lips by never uttering them but with that reverence with which you wifh you may be capable of uttering them upon your death bed.

If, by any further argument, we can prevail upon you to difcharge this duty, let us draw, from the behaviour of the world, one motive which, perhaps, will have its influence with you, for confider, that of all the rules enforcing a polite demeanour, probably not one is to be found but what comes recommended to us through the gofpel, thus a bow or curtfey is the token of a humble fervant, and the fame may be advanced refpecting every other indication of politenefs. What then does politenefs dictate on the article of fpeaking?— That we fhould apologize for barely mentioning an abfent perfon, when we tell him afterwards we introduced his name, how then fhould we excufe ourfelves if we had mentioned him with difrefpect? Much more then, how can we excufe ourfelves to God for mentioning his name without refpect? We cannot ftand excufed; much lefs then have we any thing to fay in our defence for mentioning his name with difrefpect

respect and scorn. Oh thou who art entitled,
as the psalmist tells us, reverend and holy,
give us grace to recollect that, of a certainty,
the time will come, when we shall wish to
call upon thy name, as on a name of hope and
consolation, till which time let us, as servants
were of old distinguished by their masters'
names impressed upon their foreheads, ever act
as if thy name, the name of our celestial master, were inscribed there likewise: then, in
conversation, shall we keep our tongues from
every prophanation of thy name; it will not
issue from our lips when any circumstance of
wonder or surprise takes place, but, when pronounced, will be the witness of our confidence
in God, and of our hope that we shall gain the
succour of his grace and power. We shall not
then be subject to the menace he subjoins to
his commandment, that he will not hold the
swearer guiltless, but become partakers of the
promise, joined by David, speaking in the
spirit, to his invitation of invoking him, when
overwhelmed in trouble, namely: that in
mercy he will hear us. Hear, oh God, our
supplications, when we call upon thee, in the
name of Jesus Christ, &c.

THE

THE HYMN.

OH God, who rul'ft above the fky,
How glorious is thy pow'r, how high!
How reverend too the homage fhown,
Of faints collected round thy throne!

Grant therefore that my tongue, thro' grace,
May ne'er thy name in talk debafe,
That name, which dying, e'en the beft
Of men for mercy fhall atteft.

Oh Jefus, Saviour of mankind!
How full of pity was thy mind,
When thou affumedft mortal breath
To fave us from eternal death!

Grant too thy name I may revere,
That name thro' which when death is near,
And rifing fears the heart appal,
On God, for mercy, I fhall call.

SERMON

SERMON XXX.

ON THE FOURTH COMMANDMENT.

EXODUS XX. V. 8.

Remember the fabbath day, to keep it holy.

WE begin this exhortation by addreffing
more particularly thofe among our
hearers whom their parents have thought fit to
place for education in academies or boarding
fchools, obferving, as a fort of introduction,
that fuppofing—and the fuppofition, we are
certain, will be ftriking, as the phrafe is, on a
ftring that conftantly affords their little minds
a deal of pleafant mufic,-being, as they are,
like other children, fonder of a little recreation
than much ftudy—that fuppofing any parent of
their fellow ftudents, coming on a vifit to them,
do but, as the cuftom is, prevail upon their
governefs, or mafter, to allow them the re-
mainder of the day for entertainment, in the
way themfelves think fitting, we obferve, in
fuch cafe, (we repeat) they do not, all at once,

forget

forget the friend to whom they owe their paſ-
time. On the other hand, they look as if they
echoed the expreſſion of a certain Latin writer*;
which expreſſion, if we liberally turn it into
Engliſh, may run thus. *Oh what a charming
man, or woman, he, or ſhe, muſt be, to whom
we owe this holiday.*

Or, to employ another figure, and comprize
you all together, little hearers, let but any of
your friends, relations, or acquaintance, living
in the country, ſend your parents, as a preſent,
ſuch good things intended for their table as the
country every where abounds with, you ſit
down with chearful hearts and pleaſant countenances, when the meal provided you is ready,
and forget not, during your repaſt, to drink
the health of him that, as we ſay in common,
is the founder of it

Now, dear little friends and hearers, both
theſe figures may be uſeful to you in the ſubject we are come to. Were we talking to a
congregation, ſuch as meet together in our
churches, we are ſenſible it would not be allowed us to attempt inſtructing them by ſuch a
method, they would look for ſolid argument,

* VIRGIL, in his firſt Bucolic, Deus hoc nobis otium fecit,

and

and fuch as fhould be uttered in a ftyle moft
fuited to the gravity, folemnity, and facred nature of the bufinefs in difcuffion, but your
tender age, and confequently inexperience, will
permit fome deviation from the ufual language
of inftruction. Your fimplicity is not to be
addreffed in fuch a ftyle, as thofe who are arrived to years of perfect judgment, look for,
and your playfulnefs of character may not improperly be talked to in a playfulnefs of ftyle.

We fay then, both thefe figures are in point;
that is, not out of place upon the prefent fubject: for that holiday, and that repaft, may be
a fubftitute, or reprefentative, of that feventh
day, according to the Jewifh difpenfation, but
according to the Chriftian fyftem, of that firft,
you are commanded to diftinguifh from the
other fix. But how, that is to fay, by what
behaviour are you to diftinguifh it? By fuch
as is moft fuited to the views of him that inftituted it Now, he that inftituted it, is God,
and when he did fo, he commanded we fhould
keep it holy. Keep it therefore holy, little
children, and confider, that in fome fort, as
the friend who, as we have already mentioned,
has procured you fome releafe from ftudy in
your fchool, or fome good thing to pleafe your

                                    palate,

palate, would have reafon to complain, if, while you were made happy by his gift, you did not think of him, the giver, fo too, but with infinitely greater reafon to complain, would God confider you ungrateful, if, while you were paffing what is called the fabbath, which in every meaning of the word muft be confeffed a holiday, you fhould not think of him by whom the fabbath was firft founded, and who therefore gave it you.

For if the fabbath be not, in reality, a holiday, (a *holiday*, we fay, pronouncing it as you yourfelves are ufed to do) what is? God fays, that in it you fhall do no kind of work, your fon or daughter, man or woman fervant, cattle, or the ftranger in your houfe. Now, little children, think if any friend, like him we have fuppofed already, were to tell you that to-morrow, neither you nor any one of your companions fhould be troubled with the work of ftudy; think, we fay, if, under fuch a fuppofition, you would not fet down to-morrow, in your pleafed imagination, for a holiday? The fabbath, therefore, is a holiday; and you are bound, upon the fabbath, to abftain from every labour which, in general, may be done on any other day.

But

But this is not enough; the fabbath is not
only *that*, but holy likewife, for indeed it
would not in the leaft promote God's views,
when he ordained the fabbath, that mankind
fhould keep it as a day of reft. Such reft, if
reft alone were to diftinguifh Sunday from the
other days that conftitute the week, would be
offenfive in God's fight. The fabbath day
muft, therefore, be kept holy, and fo far from
being fet apart for reft, we are commanded to do
every virtuous deed for which an opportunity
prefents itfelf, and fuch, dear children, is our
duty, that provided any of us have an ox, or
afs, that falls into a pit upon the Sunday,
we are bound to pull it out. Much more then,
upon fuch a day, are we enjoined to help our
fellow creatures, to do all the good we can, to
practice charity, which laft is, in particular, a
fervice done to God, fo much fo that we cannot do him any other · and, in fhort, to reft
from fervile labour only, and be earneftly employed in works that have God's glory, and the
benefit of human nature for their object.

In the firft, the fecond, and the third commandment, or in all, except the fourth, that
teach us what our duty is to God, we are acquainted with his law, and blindly muft we

pay

pay him our obedience: for the firſt commandment is a declaration only of his will;
the ſecond, though it has a promiſe in it of ex-
tending mercy, as it ſays, to thouſands, if they
love him and perform his ſeveral commandments, yet it awes us with a dreadful menace,
namely, of his being an avenging, that is,
jealous God, and viſiting the fathers in their
children, to the firſt, the ſecond, third, and
following generation, of all thoſe that love
him, and the third, without a promiſe, has a
threat, that he will never hold him guiltleſs
that ſhall take his name in vain. To keep
theſe three commandments, we may be induced,
we ſay, by fear, to pay a blind obedience; and in
ſuch a manner are they couched, that God
might well declare them to the Jewiſh people,
while it thundered, and the mountain burnt
with fire; but in the fourth, we can ſee nothing but God's love, and therefore no conſideration ſhould prevail upon us not to keep it.
Not to keep it, did we ſay? Such words ex-
preſs but poorly what we meant to tell you
ſhould prevail upon us not to keep it with a
joyful boſom; for, remark, theſe following
words, that make a part of the commandment:
" On the ſabbath you ſhall do no work, your
" ſon

" fon or daughter, man or woman fervant,
" cattle, or the ftranger, in your houfe "
Thefe various claffes comprehend the whole
creation, and the fabbath is thus found a friend
to man, for every one, including even the
meaneft, fhall have reft on fuch a day   But
what we notice moft of all is, that word, *cattle*.
God extends his fatherly affection to the brute
creation.   And fuppofing any one fhould afk,
with the apoftle, " What, does God take care
" of oxen ?" God, from Horeb, while it burns
with fire, and in the midft of thunder, fhall
declare himfelf their friend, as well as maker.
They, together with the whole creation of
brute creatures, fhall be every fabbath day re-
leafed from toil, that is, fuppofing their whole
life were placed before them in feven equal
parts, they fhall have one, as well as what
they pafs away in fleeping, to be wholly at
their eafe.   Think, little hearers, if, by this
proceeding, God does not appear a bounteous
parent.   Do you love your earthly parents?
You will anfwer, yes.   And why? Becaufe,
you will again make anfwer, they love you.
And do you every thing they bid you? Yes.
It is indeed your duty; but why fo? Becaufe
they have a right to bid you.   Your replies are
rational,

rational, and worthy of thofe filial feelings that fhould occupy your little hearts. Love then your heavenly father, for he loves his whole creation; and on that account, loves you. Keep too the fabbath holy, for he bids you do fo, and has much more right to bid you, than thofe parents whofe authority you all acknow-ledge.

But as yet, we have not finifhed; for we need not tell not you the commandment has much more. Which here, among you, has the tendereft parents. Underftand us properly, we mean to afk which here among you has fuch parents as are moft folicitous to make thofe children, which the providence of God already has beftowed upon them, truly happy, happy for the prefent, and in future happy likewife, temper-ing their indulgence and parental tendernefs which might perhaps be prejudicial to you, with authority and reafon, that inevitably muft be ferviceable to you. Happy he or fhe that has fuch parents! What then is their way of governing? To you, we fpeak, good child that are fo happy. Do you not difcover that their government is fometimes what fome tender parents would call hard? that they difpenfe their orders, and will not be argued with? that they

they inform you they would be obeyed? that
what they look for, is fubmiffion, not remon-
ftrance? But your God, as you may find in his
commandment, condefcends to let you know
the reafon why you fhould obey him, fince, by
way of fhowing you the reafonablenefs of keeping holy, as he fays, his fabbath, or refraining
from all fervile work thereon, he adds · *for in
the period of fix days, the Lord made Heaven and
earth, the fea with all things in them, and repofed
upon the feventh, on which account he bleffed it.*

The commandment is addreffed to every one,
who has at any time been prefent at the preaching of this exhortation : and the duty it enfor-
ces is adapted to both fexes. To obferve the
fabbath day, and keep it holy, is incumbent
upon every individual. Such a virtue, therefore, is not one of thofe which fome may ven-
ture to affert was never meant for females to
obferve. A certain ancient writer, and that
ancient writer is Theucydides, has told us that
the female fex were not defigned by Heaven to
fhine in many virtues that are fuited to the male
creation ; but that men were born for action
and the world, while women are intended for
repofe and folitude. Such arguments might
poffibly hold good, if we were heathens now,

as when this ancient lived. Then valour in
the field of battle, and ability to guide in council, were the only virtues, but the virtues of the
chriftian world are fuited to both fexes; fince
the heart alone God looks to, for the practice
of them. You have every one a heart. You
are required to have no other God excepting
God, who rules in Heaven, to venerate his
name in converfation, to refpect and reverence
your parents, to commit no murder, to abo-
minate adultery, to fteal from no one, never
to bear evidence againft your neighbour falfely,
and to covet no man's property. All thefe are
virtues to be practifed by both fexes, and fo
likewife is the confecration of the fabbath.
Be it therefore no lefs confecrated to God's
worfhip by the female, than male world; and
the intention of this exhortation will be fully
anfwered

One word more, before we finifh. Such
muft be allowed the imbecility of human nature, that if ever fpeaking with the authority of
mafters we proclaim our orders, they enforce
one duty only, but God's orders comprehend
at once a multitude of others. Oh what labour to acquire that knowledge, which is neceffary for the future man of learning, or well

VOL. II.　　　　K　　　　educated

educated woman! Write as well as ever penman did, and yet you will not therefore be expert or ready at arithmetic: the art of dancing will not make you a musician, neither will a skill in managing the needle, qualify you for the pencil: and the same is to be said of all the sciences, considered two and two, in which, industrious teachers more particularly cannot but experience the propriety of what the apostle says, though speaking on another subject, namely, that provided they desire to see the improvement of their scholars, they must never yield to difficulties, but give precept upon precept, here a line and there a line, &c. But the science of salvation has not this discouragement or stumbling block athwart the way of those who would pursue it, for be perfect in one law of God, and then you cannot but have made great progress in the all. If it were otherwise, poor children, hard would be your situation in particular! If, for example's sake, before you could be virtuous or acquainted with your duty to your parents, to each other, and to God, you were obliged to treasure in your little heads the sum and substance of the fifty two discourses in this manual. They are all indeed on different duties, and those duties must be

every

every one obferved, if you would be good children but let God's effectual grace inftruct you
to accomplifh only one, and you will hardly fail of making great proficience in the others.
We repeat then once again, and finifh with the
obfervation · keep the fabbath holy, or abftain
from fervile work thereon, that on the other-
hand, you may employ yourfelves in every
work of righteoufnefs, and then, fince you will
do fo, as the fcripture fays for confcience' fake
toward God, that confcience will inftruct you
in the duty of the fifth, the fixth, the feventh
commandment, and in fhort of all the others.
May this grace and this inftruction be your portion, little children, for the fake of Jefus Chrift,
and may his prophecy, refpecting your undoubt-
ed claim to Heaven, as children, never be reverfed by the unhappy confequence of fin, when
you attain to years of manhood, or the feafon
of old age. Hear us, oh father, through the
fame, our Lord and Saviour Jefus Chrift, &c.

K 2   THE

THE HYMN.

THIS is the day, by God's beheft
Ordained for man and brute to reft:
  For brute, that from his fix days' toil
    Some refpite he may know,
  So too for man, but who the while
    His gratitude fhould fhow
For benefits received, or fpend
In prayer the day to his almighty friend.

Then let us God's great love fulfil,
The gracious purpofe of his will,
  From labour may our cattle reft
    In undifturb'd repofe,
  But for ourfelves, with grateful breaft,
    To him, the fource whence flows
All happinefs, our praifes pay,
Or on bent knees before him, lowly pray.

SERMON

SERMON XXXI.

ON THE FIFTH COMMANDMENT.

EXODUS XX. V. 12.

Honour thy father and thy mother, that thy days may be long upon the land which the Lord thy God giveth thee.

GREAT God! And is it possible, dear little children, you that have so great a love for, and of course so highly honour those good parents who first gave you life, and by whose prayers, which many of them offer up incessantly in your behalf to him that is our common father, or at least by whose continual assiduities on earth, and in this state of being, which they all exert to make you happy, you are everlastingly deriving blessings from them—is it possible, we say, and more particularly after the whole world had been destroyed, or drowned by the waters of a flood, for sins that had their origin in filial disobedience, among

K 3 other

other crimes fuggefted by the devil   Once more, is it poffible, we fay, that, fince the deluge, fin had fo increafed among mankind, that God fhould have confidered it expedient to enact a law, intended to make children honour, as it fays, their parents, and abftain from the commiffion of that fin which the commandment was intended to abolifh, and in which there is an equal portion of ingratitude to thofe the offenders always have in view before them, with rebellion to that framer of the law, whom they have not, we muft confefs, before them, but whofe right to iffue fuch a law is incontefftible, or not to be difputed, from the tokens of his greatnefs fo diffufively, that is to fay, fo widely fcattered round about us?

Yes, dear little children, notwithftanding the effects which we may naturally think a deluge would have operated on the mind of finners, it is poffible that God fuppofed it neceffary to proclaim a law, enjoining the performance of that duty which is due from children to their parents, for, affuredly, there muft be fome among you that remember reading in the Bible of that Canaan, fon of Noah, who, together with his family, confifting altogether of eight perfons, were the only individuals God thought

proper

proper to preserve from the destruction of the
deluge Canaan, not perhaps a twelvemonth
after, as we read, was so irreverent, as to mock
his father, who, in consequence of having
drank too largely of the produce of a vineyard
he had lately planted, grew intoxicated, and lay
prostrate on the ground, in such a situation as
is natural to think was very unbecoming Canaan saw him in this situation, and, instead
of throwing over him some covering to conceal
his nakedness, told Shem and Japheth, his
two elder brothers, what he had observed,
and, as we may suppose, with circumstan-
ces of derision, or, at least, in such a manner as was little suited to the reverence due
from children to their parents. It was certainly a sin in Noah to be drunken, but it was not
for his child to reprehend or blame him, much
less then, expose his fault to others with derision. From this little history, which we have
on record, of unchild-like conduct to a parent,
at a time when the offender had a deluge fresh
in his remembrance, (for you recollect he was
preserved from being drowned in it) do you
learn, dear little hearers, to respect your parents, lest the punishment of Canaan should
become your portion, but which punishment,

the

the plan of our difcourfe will not permit us to enlarge on now, though you are all apprized thereof, if you have ever read the Bible, and, inftead of ridiculing their behaviour, though perhaps it may be blamable, do you conceal their guilt, and fave them from becoming objects of derifion to their neighbours. Shem and Japheth, Canaan's brothers, in their piety did this, when they both took a garment, laid it on their fhoulders, and went backward, fo that they might throw it over their intoxicated father, and conceal his nakednefs; which, far from imitating Canaan in his conduct by deriding it, they would not even look at.

This, however, you will fay, was but a trifling fin, and only one, fince we can find no other inftance mentioned of this Canaan's difobedience. Be perfuaded, little ones, however, that no fin can be confidered trifling in God's fight. Such an idea will contribute very much to keep you all within the limits of your duty, while the other is the caufe that thoufands every day are conftantly committing fin: but if you wifh to have another inftance, and extracted from the Bible likewife, of this filial difobedience, greater than the former, you may find it in the book of Judges, in the four-
teenth

teenth chapter; after which you may inform
yourself of the unhappy confequences which
the offender's crime was followed by, though
not *immediately*, yet mediately at leaft, but
which, no more than Canaan's punifhment,
fhall we, at prefent, fpeak of. Samfon, whofe
fad ftory fome of you, no doubt, dear children, are acquainted with, was once the hope
and confolation of his parents, and intended,
by God's providence, to prove the friend and
faviour of his countrymen, when otherwife the
enemy would have oppreffed them grievoufly.
Unhappy parents! little did you think at what
a great expence and peril to your fon this friendfhip and falvation were at laft to be effected:
but your Samfon difobeyed you, he rejected
the advice of thofe who would have fhown
themfelves the guides of his ungovernable youth,
and the Almighty's judgments are not to be
called in queftion. Samfon grew to years of
manhood, under the affection and fond fafeguard of his parents, and the Lord was with
him but, at laft, he chanced to caft his eye
upon a beautiful young woman, daughter to a
Philiftine, when, captivated at the fight, and
not confidering that the Philiftines were fore
oppreffors of his country, over which they held

K 5 dominion,

dominion, he informed his father of the inter-
view, and *bade* him, (for the story does not tell
us he *requested* what he wished for) bade him,
we repeat, obtain her for his wife, on which
his father asked him, if among the females of
his country there was no young woman—that
he needs must go and marry with his enemies?
This question comprehended, certainly, good
counsel or advice, but Samson, with the rash
impetuous temper of a youth, that can at once
forget the duty owing to a father, and conceive
himself much wiser than a parent, answers in
a sort of passion, *get her for me for she pleases me.*
As much as if he had directly told him, he
knew nothing of the matter, and that, notwithstanding every thing a father had to urge
against a match so ill-proportioned, he would
marry her his heart was set on

Hitherto, however, little friends, we have
said nothing more than is sufficient to surprise
your generous nature, and perhaps you say on
the occasion, every one expressing his own
thoughts, had Canaan's father been my father,
I would never have exposed, as he did, the
old man, but saved him from the ridicule
of others. And had Samson's father been my
father, I would gladly have attended to his
counsel,

counfel, and not married, as he did, a woman
from the country of my enemies. Oh cherifh
thefe fair notions in your hearts, dear children,
probably, becaufe thefe two were wanting, or
deficient, on this head, did they incur the punifhment that afterward befel them. Hitherto,
dear children, we repeat, we have faid nothing
more than is fufficient to furprife your generous
nature, but are now to fhock it by relating the
behaviour of a fon, in no refpect lefs fhameful,
than if any one of you fhould turn a father, or
a mother, out of doors, without even food or
clothes, and bid them howl out their complaining
to the winds, or fend a perfon after to affaffinate
or murder them. This fon was Abfalom,
whofe ftory you may find related in the 13th
of the fecond book of Samuel, and four following chapters. Abfalom was cherifhed by his
father David, and the love with which he
viewed him was fo great, that even after this
unnatural fon had treacheroufly killed his brother Amnon, he forgave him. But this love
afforded him much furer means of proving far
more treacherous, for being pardoned, and
re-called to dwell in fafety with his father, at
Jerufalem, he there complicated the abominable
purpofe of his heart, and, by contriving to

feduce

feduce the affections of the people, raifed an in--
furrection, and drove out the author of his life,
to wander in the wildernefs ; and *that* not only
robbed of his dominions, but reduced to trem-
ble for his life , for when a certain friend of Abfalom, obferving David in his haplefs fituation,
curfed, and otherwife infulted him ; and when
the faithful Abifhai would have fmitten off his
head,nay afked the king's permiffion for that purpofe, David, utterly infenfible of every outrage,
when he thought of that much greater outrage
perpetrated by a fon, made anfwer,*What have I to
do with thee, thou fon of Zeruiah ? Let him curfe ;
for doth not my own fon, even he that iffued from
thefe bowels, feek my life?* Ah, little auditors ! could
any father merit fuch unnatural treatment from
his fon ? but more particularly one fo good , good,
you will fay to all, when you have heard what
we are going now to tell you. It appears,
that David being hunted by the Philiftines, was
fore oppreffed for want of wherewithal to quench
his thirft, and faid, with fomething of an ex-
clamation *Oh that any one would get me drink!*
On which three officers, on peril of their lives,
procured him water.   But when told at what
a rifque they had befriended him, he would not
drink it , faying, *God forbid I fhould refrefh my-*
                                        felf

felf with what your lives might very poffibly have paid for! So he poured it out before the Lord. We have related this to fhow you how enormous muft have been the fin of Abfalom's revolt againft fo good a father, for the man who could conduct himfelf thus kindly to his officers, muft have particularly loved his children.

Having thus related the exceeding wickednefs of Abfalom, we afk if his behaviour does not fhock your nature? Canaan's crime was only the tranfaction of a minute: Samfon's was much greater; and yet, after all, did not fo properly proclaim a criminal, as foolifh difpofition, and alas! among mankind, who has it in his power to boaft of being wife at all times: but the wretched Abfalom was wicked beyond all example, and contained the very root, if we may fay fo, of iniquity, within him. Liften therefore to his punifhment, as well as that of Samfon and the other · for of that we are to fpeak, and with it end our fermon; namely, with the punifhment of difobedient children. Once more then, we fay, dear children, liften and oppofe this punifhment in your ideas to that length of days God promifes he will beftow on thofe who honor, as he fays, their parents. Abfalom was caught up by his hair, as he was

riding

riding under a great oak , that hair whofe beauty was before remarked by all that faw the youth, was changed at length into an engine to deftroy him , for while thus fufpended between heaven and earth, an officer belonging to his father, three times ftabbed him to the heart, and he expired.   This was the punifhment of Abfalom's unfilial conduct.   Samfon, by defpifing the advice of his, allied himfelf in marriage to a woman who was taken from him , after which, that is to fay when he cohabited with an abandoned female, fhe reduced him to fo fad a fituation, by betraying him to his relentlefs enemies, that having had his eyes put out, and being forced to labour like a beaft of burthen, life became a trouble to him ; fo that being brought before the Philiftine great men or nobles, to afford them fport and paftime, he conceived the notion of a defperate revenge upon them, which his ftrength of body, you will fee, enabled him to compafs · for while 'propt againft two pillars, over which the roof, where they were met, was turned (moft likely) archwife, he grafped nard, and with his utmoft ftrength affaying to pull down the fabric, uttered fomething like a prayer, as follows let me die with the Philiftines, when behold ' the roof in

every

every part gave way, and falling, buried upwards
of three thoufand Philiftines, together with himfelf, beneath its ruins. This too was the punifhment of Samfon's difobedience to his father;
and by fuch means was the prophecy, which
the Almighty's fpirit had declared before his
birth, as well as by the former mifchief he had
done the Philiftines, to be fulfilled, while Canaan, for the ridicule and fcorn to which he would
have fo unthinkingly expofed a father, drew
upon himfelf the old man's maledi&ion. *Curfed,*
were his words, *be Canaan · he fhall be the fervant
of his brethren.* This, in fine, was Canaan's
punifhment for difobedience to his father.

Now let none of you, dear children, think
that even the leaft of thefe three punifhments,
the punifhment of Canaan, is a trifle; but
confider, that a parent's curfe, a curfe pronounced upon you by thofe lips that nature would in-
ftru&t to blefs you, may be followed by the moft
diftreffing confequences. But the fubje&t of
this curfe, we mean not to enlarge on. In the
earlier ages it might feem a father was invefted
with fome fort of privilege to curfe, and God
was ufed to hear his curfes: but thefe prefent
times afford no inftance of that nature. We
might therefore lofe our labour, fhould we warn
you

you upon peril of a father's curfe, to fhun the
guilt of difobedience to him. parents being,
after, all unjuft, and liable to err themfelves:
nor will we feek to terrify you, by the punifhment of Ablalom, into the duty of refpecting
thofe who gave you birth, becaufe it may be
faid that his unhappy fate was brought about
through accident, but by the miferable fate of
Samfon, we adjure you to be duteous children;
to remember what God fays, as in the fifth
commandment. " Honour thofe that are
" your parents, that your days may long con-
" tinue in the land," and to conceive you
hear the words of Samfon tingling in your ear,
whenever you are tempted to be difobedient,
namely, " let me die with the Philiftines."

For what does that expreffion, *let me die with
the Philiftines*, mean? It means· " Ah me! I
" fcorned the counfel of a father, who affection-
" ately loved me, and rufhed haftily into a mar-
" riage that has been my ruin. I have forfeited
" my reputation. I have loft my God, who had
" beforehand promifed me a length of days, if I
" would honour or revere my parents In a
" ftate fo wretched, what have I to hope for?
" Nothing Life itfelf is grown a mifery to me.
" Let me end it then at once." Dear children,

do

do you hear this forrowful complaint? The criminal avows his difobedience, but defpairs. Methinks, we hear the wretched Judas tell the priefts and elders he had finned, but fee him afterward depart and hang himfelf.

Oh heavenly father, of thy mercy fill this little flock affembled in thy prefence, with that grace which may infpire them with a proper fpirit of obedience to their parents, and inftruct them that no facrifice upon their part can be too great for all the pains their education cofts them. Are they not young plants, which thou thyfelf haft planted, trufting to their parents the great work of rearing them till they attain maturity? To their maturity let them attain, beneath fuch cultivation, and at laft, when by thy will the time is come for the departure of their parents, may they pour out their laft breath in the embraces of their children. Guard them from the fin of filial difobedience, and if any one here prefent, after all, unhappily fhould yield to bad examples or temptations of the evil fpirit, be ftill merciful, oh father, to them, notwithftanding they offend as well againft the light of nature, as thy grace. Let them difcern the enormous nature of their fin and ftill more merciful, preferve them from

defpair

defp.. in their conviction, fo that imitating the repentance of the prodigal thy bleffed fon has left on record for our learning, let them go in deep contrition to their parents, and confeffing then in actual conduct, fay they are no longer worthy to be called their children, but intreat reception as hired fervants. Then no doubt, fhall their deferving parents, glad of fuch return, receive them as the prodigal s did him bring hither the beft robe, a ring, and fhoes, fhall be then cry. Kill inftantly the fatted calf, and let us banquet or rejoice. Vouchfafe oh God it may be fo, with every one fo miferable as to imitate the prodigal in his behaviour to fond parents, but fo happy, in the fequel, as to fee the crime of his behaviour, and return. This we requeft, through Jefus Chrift, &c.

THE HYMN.

GREAT pleafure, oh Lord,
  Have they who fulfil
Thy facred commands
  And follow thy will:

And

And if fitting honour
  Our parents we pay,
No less satisfaction
  Ourselves have than they.

Then let us, oh Lord,
  Our parents revere;
Obey them tho' life,
  And love while we fear:

Left Canaan's hard fortune,
  Or Abfalom's fate,
Or Samfon's, or worse, our
  Rebellion await.

.

SERMON

SERMON XXXII.

ON THE EIGHTH COMMANDMENT.

EXODUS XX. V. 15.

Thou shalt not steal.

HONESTY, dear children, is the best, that is most gainful, policy. So says the proverb, just as if the framer of it had informed us, that whoever would be cunning, and draw profit from his cunning, should reject all knavish dispositions, and be upright, so that the commandment we are now to preach on, is addressed much rather to mankind as they have dealings with each other in a state of nature, than to beings who are meant for heaven, when, by obeying the commandments of their maker, they have made themselves, in some sort, worthy of it. With that maker, therefore, let *us* say to every one of you here present, dear disciples, what the eighth commandment says, *videlicet· Thou shalt not steal.* While other children, having no one to inculcate in their

bosom

bofom any principles of virtue, or neglecting to improve fuch principles as may have previoufly been planted in them; while thofe children, we repeat, purloin or pilfer from their fellows, *thinking* what they get will make them happier in themfelves, do you, upon the other hand, good children, that have parents anxious to endow you with a virtuous education, be as anxious, on your part, to fecond or affift their views, which are directed to your benefit, and confcientioufly refpect the property of every one about you, *knowing*, that by fuch refpect, you will be happier in yourfelves, than all the little matters of another, fhould they come into your hands improperly, could make you.

How, indeed, can the affair be otherwife? for look, dear children, round you, and take notice what a multitude of comforts, or good things, have been provided for the ufe of man, by the immediate bounty of that God who has impofed, or laid upon us, among other prohibitions, the commandment of not ftealing. See yourfelves furrounded with a hoft of objects that delight the eye and other fenfes. Now all thefe, as we have juft now mentioned, came from God. It would be, then, abfurd to fancy that the power, who has performed fo

much

much for your advantage, should restrain you
by a law which, if you kept it, would not
make you happy. Would your parents treat
you in so unaccountable a manner? They provide you all the good things in their power,
and every rule they give for your behaviour, is
intended for your happiness. It would not be
confident in them to be so affectionate on one
hand, and so harsh upon the other. From their
love then, and its consequences, may be drawn
a sketch, though but a sketch, and *that* exceedingly imperfect likewise, of the love evinced
by the Almighty.—Jesus Christ has authorised
us to assert thus much *for if*, says the Redeemer, *you that are*, as he expressed it, *wicked,
give good gifts to all your children, how much
more shall not your heavenly Father give good gifts
to such as ask him?* Now, to give good gifts,
and issue a commandment that would render us
unhappy, is an inconsistency. The eighth
commandment consequently is a law contri-
buting to make men happy. Keep it therefore
in your tender time of life, dear children. It
will make you happy, and not that alone,
but it will make you rich, if any system of behaviour can have that effect.

For

For God forbid that fraud, however it may sometimes prosper, should enrich mankind, or even make them comfortable in their situation. In this part of our discourse, let us address all those among you that, in future, have to make fortune by such talents as your education in the world is to procure, and afterwards point out the advantages resulting from an observation of the eighth commandment, so superior as they are to all the benefits resulting from a violation of it, for consider what the psalmist says: the psalmist was a king, and had it in his power, no doubt, to make the fortunes of as many as he undertook to patronize, but those alone, as he informs us, should obtain admission to his presence, and the privilege of waiting on him who were upright in their dealings. His expression is, " Mine eyes shall be " upon the faithful in the land, that they may " dwell with me." And why upon the faithful? But because there cannot be a greater treasure to the master of a family, than the possession of an honest servant. Now, dear children, in the world of business we are all, in some sort, servants to each other, and this honesty induces masters to retain their servants; so that, in such service, they have every opportunity

portunity of making, what we call, their fortune. Thus, though very briefly, have we
shown you the advantages annexed to honesty Now see the consequences fraud is commonly attended with but why enumerate
them? You have frequently heard mention of
such things as jails, or prisons: well then,
know, that notwithstanding every county in
the kingdom (and in England there are two
and fifty counties) has a prison in it, to which
number must be added many others, they are
generally full of miserable, and too frequently
abandoned, people, who, beforehand, having
loved a life of indolence and theft, are waiting,
while we speak at present, the award of law
on their dishonesty Of these abandoned people, the least guilty will receive the scourge of
some unfeeling executioner upon their flesh,
amid a multitude of scoffers, and perhaps atone
for their offences by additional imprisonment,
or loss of freedom Others, torn from their
relations, to consume the remnant of their lives
in banishment, will be transported to a country, whence, unless by something like a miracle in their behalf, not one among them will
return to those relations, while the rest, as being most of all abandoned, (horrible to think of,

and

and more fo to mention,) will be publicly expofed upon a fcaffold, and refign their lives for
violating laws which were enacted to preferve
the property of individuals from fuch robbers.

Which, then, of thefe two fo different fituations would you wifh, dear children, to appear
in? Doubtlefs you would chufe that others,
having places or employments to beftow,
might have it in their power to fay of you,
with David, when they thought upon your
honeft dealing—it is you fhall be my fervant.
Bend your ftudy then to merit fuch a character, and to avoid the imputation of difhonefty,
left that unhappy fortune, namely, ftripes in-
flicted on your body, with imprifonment, or,
very likely, exile from your friends and native
country, if not death with ignominy, fhould
become your lot, for what are you, that if you
yield to thofe temptations which may poffibly
befet you, as before they have befet fo many,
you fhould hope to fave yourfelf from the unhappy confequences law annexes to difhoneft
actions. Poffibly you may confider, that thefe
folemn warnings do your character no honour,
fince we deem it probable you may be brought
to the commiffion of thofe actions. No, dear
children, we have no fuch thoughts, but, as

on one hand, granting you had fhown yourfelves fo guilty, we would then endeavour to alle-
viate, or excufe, the enormity of what had
been committed, for the fake of thofe we are
fo fond of, fo too, for an equal reafon, on the
other hand, that we may fhow you our affection by thefe falutary warnings, we fuppofe
more poffible than prefent circumftances may
allow us to conceive will happen. Take, then,
in good part, the advice we give you ; it is
wholly for your benefit, not ours , and be upon
your guard againft the leaft temptations to the
leaft difhonefty that poffibly can be committed.
Think it not enough that you avoid occafions
of purloining from another what may injure him
confiderably, but be this your firft idea, namely, that the crime is in God's law forbidden.
Say not, " if I put my hand upon this thing,
" or that, belonging to my friend, or other
" perfon, it will injure him but little, while
" the benefit to me will be immenfe." When
once you enter upon arguments, you are no
more a child, but forfeit the fimplicity annexed
to fuch a ftate, and which is better far than all
the cunning you can manifeft, for children do
not fhow their lovelinefs by arguing with their
betters in the world, and much lefs then with
                                        God,

God, but by obeying fuch injunctions as are laid upon them.

Thefe injunctions, in the ftricteft fenfe, it is an eafy thing for you, dear children, to ob-ferve. Your ftate in life, or rather that of your indulgent parents, who can purchafe you fo many comforts and conveniencies, exempts you from temptations to difhonefty; by which it comes to pafs, that you are under no necef-fity of feeking to fupply your wants, but you, that while we fpeak, we think we fee before us, children of diftrefs and poverty, what fhall we fay to you? This doctrine of foregoing every fpecies of temptation to the act of fraud, and more particularly when the lofs is trifling to another, and the benefit accruing from it great to you, is haid, and which of you, as the difciple fays to Jefus Chrift, can bear it? What, when you have neither fhoes nor ftock-ings to put on, and when your clothes are fcarcely any thing but rags and tatters, while the chilling winter, rain, hail, froft or fnow affails your fhivering bodies, fhall God write it down in his eternal book a fin, if, to de-fend your trembling nakednefs from the unpity-weather, you make free with fomething that is laid up in the ftores of fuch as have fo many

L 2   coats,

coats, or garments, and lofe nothing by the
deed, fince what they do not wear they cannot
feel the want of? When you fuffer the extreme
of hunger, and would think yourfelves partaking of a feaft, if happier children would beftow
upon your famifhed need thofe crumbs they
fling away, fhall it be thought a fin in you,
if from an overflowing table you purloin a cruft
which otherwife the dogs beneath their board
would have? Yes, poor forfaken little ones,
who fuffer for the indolence, at leaft, if not
the vice of thofe that gave you being, though
we pity your condition, we muft anfwer, that
to get yourfelves relief againft the law of God,
would be a fin. What further can we fay?
We wifh, alas! we could, with honefty, do
more than recommend you to God's providence.
—the power who fatisfies the raven when it
calls upon him, and who feeds not only the
large oftrich, but replenifhes the air with atoms
to fubfift or nourifh the leaft fly that wings its paffage through it, will not, in the end, abandon
you. Truft, then, in God, and fince, as you will
come to know hereafter, life does not fo much
confift in having food to eat, or raiment to put
on, as in obeying the Almighty, frame your
little hearts, as the apoftle tells you, with all
diligence,

diligence, to walk like other children, happier than yourselves it may be, with respect to worldly riches, but not better, with regard to walking in the way of his commandments.

Having briefly thus addressed that portion of the rising generation whose condition is so truly to be pitied, miserable as they are, and born without the gifts of fortune, yet enjoined by human laws not only to respect those gifts in others, but commanded likewise by religion not to covet the possession of them, though they make so many happy who have all things, while themselves, upon the other hand, want all things, we return to you, more favoured of God's providence, and from the words just mentioned, of *not coveting*, draw other matter, which when we have briefly handled, we shall finish our discourse We say then, that not only has God said, you shall not steal, but added afterward, *you shall not covet either house, wife, servant, ox, or ass*: in short, *you shall not covet any thing belonging to your neighbour.* This we need not tell you is the tenth commandment, and by this, God bids you put away entirely every species of temptation to infringe or violate the eighth, by warning you against the crime of wishing to possess your neighbour's

L 3   pro-

property, in fuch a way that it may lead you to
purloin it.   On the fin of ftealing, we have faid
enough; but if, dear children, from a want of
grace, which muft inceffantly watch over you,
or fin will of neceffity infect your little hearts,
you have unwarily proceeded to the act of
picking, as your catechifm fays, and *ftealing*.
what, except evincing our affliction for the fin
you have committed, fhall we fay?   What the
apoftle Paul, in that epiftle which he wrote to
the Ephefians, faid: *let him that ftole, take care
and fteal no more*.   So that you fee, there is a
remedy for what in this refpect you may have
done amifs.   Although the fin of ftealing be a
grevious one indeed, we mean not to upbraid you,
but employ an admonition no lefs kind to you,
whofe tender age pleads greatly in excufe of
any fin you may unhappily commit, and whofe
endearing countenances no one fure can look at
and not find himfelf difarmed, when otherwife he
would have treated you with a degree of anger
(fuch we mean as fhould produce your benefit.)
Let us, we fay then, ufe an admonition no lefs
kind to you, than what St. Paul employed to
thofe who were of years fufficient to difcern the
enormity of that particular offence we have been
fpeaking of, and who, perhaps, were hardened

in

in it. *He that has already stolen, let him steal no more,* and likewise, be perfuaded that in every period of his life, this precept may redound to his advantage, if he does as it directs him, fince a true repentance never can be fet about too late. Oh God of juftice, and of mercy, who haft willed that in the laft particular, we fhould endeavour to refemble thee, by promifing that the compaffion we extend to others, fhall become the rule of that thou wilt fhow us, vouchfafe that in the firft too, we may think it not impoffible, if but affifted by thy grace and favour, to accomplifh what thou wilt confider pleafing in thy fight. This little family affembled in thy prefence, let their teacher recommend to thy protection · write thy laws upon their tender hearts, and grant that, as in others, fo in this they may obey thee, but particu'arly fave their childhood and their youth from the pernicious influence of thofe bad examples that furround them, from the bad examples of the crouded city, and, in fhort, of every quarter in the land, wherein fo many every year are facrificed to juftice. Save them from the crime and from the miferable fortune of thefe men; but of their crime, while they exprefs a due abhorrence, by the actions of their life, their perfons let them pity, and re-

L 4

plenifhed

plenifhed with the fpirit of religion, fay in their
devotion, when they kneel before thee every
night and morning, which we truft, by the di-
rection of their tutors, they will do, *preferve thou
thofe, oh God, that are appointed*, as thy prophet
fays, *to die !* Hear us, we pray thee, in behalf
of all that have departed from the way of thy
commandments, and vouchfafe to bring them
back, through Jefus Chrift, &c.

THE HYMN,

POOR people, deftitute of cloaths,
   And left without a meal,
May plead fome right to an excufe,
   When pinch'd by want, they fteal.

And yet even thefe for theft, the law
   To due difgrace will bring:
And oft the frowning judge pronounce
   Death's doom upon their fin.

But

But what, oh Lord! fhall I find out
   In my behalf, to fay,
If fcornıng thy juft laws, I fteal
   Another's right away.

I that have coftly cloaths to wear
   Wıth fuch good food to eat ,
And ın whofe perfon, therewıthal,
   So many comforts meet.

From prıde, ıf not from vırtue, then,
   Let me abhor the ways
Of knavıfh men, left death, wıth fhame,
   Abrıdge my youthful days.

SERMON

SERMON XXXIII.

ON ANGER.

EPHESIANS vi. v. 4.

Fathers, provoke not your children to wrath; but bring them up in the nurture and admonition of the Lord.

HOW happy is the heart of real friend-ship, when perhaps not lefs ingenious than induftrious in its fearch, it can affign ex-cufes for the faults of thofe it loves! Thus, at this prefent writing, is it, little friends, with us. In your deportment often do we notice, not indeed that wrath which fprings from ma-lice in the heart, and leads it on to fchemes of vengeance; but that wrath which has its origin in human weaknefs, and accuftoms you to certain little vehemencies, that in no degree become the gentlenefs of nature in the innocent and fimple ftate of childhood. Such a wrath, we fay, we often fee in your demeanour, and la-ment, that on the whitenefs of the fnow, there fhould be any thing approaching to the nature

of

of a fpot or blemifh ; and that what in children we may call the beauty, as already we
have faid, of holinefs, fhould be degraded, in
the leaft degree, by that deformity which fin
muft always be attended with ; for though thefe
little vehemencies are not, in themfelves un-
pardonable fins, yet are they real fins, and
will, if cherifhed, certainly conduct to greater;
infomuch, that he who in his childhood might
have, very eafily, been argued out of fuch an
evil, may become the fport of every furious
paffion in his manhood: and if, happily, religion, at that period, fhould be kindled in his
heart, he will difcern himfelf, in fome fort,
toffed about, like the difciples of Chrift Jefus
in their boat, when he was fleeping ; and, in
anguifh, be reduced to imitate their conduct,
when awaking him, they cried out, faying,
fave us, Lord, or we fhall perifh!

God be therefore gracious to you, little children, let us fay, as we have more than once
expreffed ourfelf already, and at no time may
the veffel of your peace be loft, or even dafhed
about, becaufe you are in want of one to fteer
it for you through the ftreights of childhood ;
fo that when you come into the open fea of
life, it may be well provided with all manner

L 6 of

of good things on board, to gain the wished-for
port : but if, for want of such a pilot in your
earlier season, or for want of having profited
by his directing hand, you should be afterward
the sport of storms, and if that anger you have
cherished in your bosom should go near to sink
your vessel, may God still be gracious to you!
May the danger you are in alarm you ! May
you cry, Lord save us, or we sink ! And may
his mercy calm the tempest, and conduct your
vessel safe into its port.

This is, however, only a digression, for
which reason we return and say, that having
noticed many of the little vehemencies you give
way to, we lamented their existence, and a
gloom diffused itself, at such a prospect, thro'
our heart, that Nature, from the very cradle,
should be thus ungovernable. But, dear little
children, let us not find fault with Nature ;
God and Nature, very often, are the same ;
and they who seek to throw on Nature all the
blame of the offences they commit, endeavour,
in another manner, to make God the cause of
those offences. Let us, therefore, not find
fault, we say, with Nature, but with Nature's
nurses, if that word may be allowed us. And
this observation brings us to repeat the text,
which

which is intended, not for thofe indeed here
prefent, but their parents, who, no doubt,
have often read and coincided with it, as con-
taining a judicious piece of counfel, though,
miftaking what is real kindnefs in a parent,
they have finned againft that council. What
then is it? Hear the words repeated: *Parents,*
for when Paul fays " fathers," he means
" mothers" likewife, *provoke not your children
to wrath, but bring them up in the nurture and
admonition of the Lord.*

And is it poffible that parents can provoke
their children thus to wrath or anger, innocent
as children are at all times in themfelves?
And if they can, muft we confefs they do fo
likewife? Yes, for to be candid, frankly muft
we own they can, and do, not actively, however, but at leaft by what is called permiffion,
by a tendernefs that will not be prevailed on to
deny them any thing. Is it a circumftance of
wonder, therefore, if their little ones, conceiving every thing fhould be allowed them, dif-
agree with every thing when, as will fometimes be the cafe, they meet with oppofition to
their humours? Do they find a door-way clofed
againft them which they thought to pafs thro'?
they will beat and thump it with the greateft
violence.

violence. Is any one difpofed to ftop them, when they fet a running?—they will hardly fail to kick him. Do they fall and hurt their face againft the ground?—a nurfe fhall be at hand to afk them for a blow, that fhe may beat it for prefuming thus to hurt her little deary. Thefe, it will perhaps be faid, are puerilities that none but infants will defcend to. Is it then a lefs degree of puerility, when older, if a pen does not produce fuch ftrokes as they would have it, they are ruffled on a fudden, and wound up into a paffion, fplit it up that moment on the table, or evince their anger in another manner? Is that violent refentment lefs to be condemned for childifhnefs, which, when an artift is at work, for inftance, with his brufh, and if it does not give the colouring he defigned it fhould, he will exert, by throwing it with indignation from him, and, perhaps, accompanying too the action with an oath?

Now, what fay thofe acquainted with a human body's ftructure, and the operation of the parts within us?—That by dint of launching out thus often into fits of paffion, what is called the *bile*, grows more and more abundant, and which great increafe of bile contributes, every day, to make fuch fits ftill more and more habitual

bitual to us. What then, little children, to
addrefs you now inftead of your miftaking parents, is it your incumbent duty to perform, if,
at a future time of life, you would not be ob-
noxious to the tyranny of anger? Your incumbent duty is no more than this: to check it in
its birth; and then, if, at a future period, men
fhould even infult you,—upon fuch a fuppofition,
far from giving way to every guft of rage, you
will be able to poffefs your fouls in patience,
no lefs great than what the elder Cato, an il-
luftrious Roman fenator, gave proof of; Cato,
we repeat, who once endured a blow which,
his hiftorian, Plutarch, tells us, an infulting
defperado, called Covinus, gave him in a full
affembly of the people. He put up with fuch
an infult, and, by no means fought the opportunity of killing, either then or afterward, his
adverfary; or evinced, in any other way, his
anger.

　You will come, we fay, dear little ones, to
this exalted pitch of heroifm, though the motive will be different, and make all the actions
of your life confiftent, which was not the cafe
with Cato; he was patient at the inftigation
of his pride, although the affertion feems a little
paradoxical, and we adduce his great example,

ple, only to convince you of the patience human nature may be brought to. Yes, we fay,
that Cato's patience fprung from pride, for
which he was fo noted, that when Ptolemy, a
king of Egypt, came to Cyprus on a vifit to
him, he would not go forth to meet the monarch, no, nor barely quit his fitting pofture
to receive him when he entered his apartment.

And why this difparity of conduct? Why,
dear little hearers, but becaufe he never had
received that nurture, and that admonition of
the Lord, which in the text is recommended.

In a word, he was a heathen, ignorant of
Jefus Chrift, from whom muft come the fource
of all our virtues; fo that having faid it is your
duty to fupprefs or check all anger in its birth,
we add, it is a further duty to conduct yourfelf, as Paul advifes the Philippians, *with all
lowlinefs and meeknefs, with long fuffering, forbearing one another in love.*

Now let us afk you, little friends and hearers,
if this lowlinefs and meeknefs, this long fuffering and forbearance of each other, as the precept fays, in love, are not precifely four fuch
virtues as feem fuited to the faculties of children. Beings of your tender age appear moft
likely to accomplifh what the apoftle orders,

who,

who, on that account, feems writing to them, and *them* only, for can men, whofe paffions have fo long been gathering ftrength by time, and who, perhaps, are proud and haughty, eafily defcend to lowlinefs and meeknefs. Is it probable that fuch as are impatient of the leaft reftraint fhould change their very conftitution, as it were, or grow long fuffering; and without a certainty of being difappointed, fhall we ftipulate that thofe who, from a notion of their own fuperior worthinefs, have been accuftomed to make no allowance for the imperfections which adhere to nature, fhall be wrought on, all at once, to make allowance for fuch imperfections, or forbear each other, as the text expreffes it, in love? No: the tranfition is not natural, and children only, that is only they, who are by nature lowly, meek, long fuffering, and forbearing, and are therefore in the way of four fuch virtues, can with eafe continue to purfue it. Grace, indeed, may operate a total change in any human being's nature, and convert the moft iniquitous or hardened into faints, but we are only to expect fuch things will come to pafs as generally happen in the world. Confidering, therefore, men in their maturity and childhood, we can teach the laft with greater probability of having our inftructions ſtructions faithfully complied with, than the firſt; ſince to the firſt we muſt addreſs ourſelves, in ſome degree, as follows: " You have left " the path of virtue, and muſt ſtrike again " into it," which is very difficult: but to the laſt, " you are by nature in the path of virtue, " and have nothing elſe to do than keep it," which is very eaſy. Hence then, what con-cluſion ſhall we draw ?—the following· that God's word is in particular the friend of chil-dren, and appears to have been wholly written for their benefit.

We ſay then, little ones, ſuppreſs, while you are little, all thoſe ſtarts of anger you may find on ſeveral occaſions riſing in you, and if now your parents were but by to hear us, we would ſay, with the apoſtle, " See that you " provoke not, as you do ſometimes, your " little ones to wrath." We grant, that if you violate the precept, it originates entirely from your love that can deny your children no one thing they aſk for· but this love is a miſ-taken love; and therefore a diſeaſe of which you ſhould be cured. Now God, as we may notice, has, for every ailment we are ſubject to, let it be bodily or mental, gracioufly ſup-plied us with a remedy, and he takes care to

place

place this remedy clofe by the ailment, as he
has in this; for if, miftaken love may caufe
fome deviation from the line of duty in the
education of your children, you have reafon
and the gofpel near at hand to rectify your love,
and tell you how much more that love will
be evinced in favour of your little ones, if you
take care to educate them in the nurture, as
our text goes on, and admonition of the Lord.
This, as we faid before, is an idea we fuggeft
to parents. We addrefs ourfelf in the re-
mainder of this exhortation, little friends, to
you, and fhall fupply you with two fketches,
which will fhow, on the comparifon of one
againft the other, how more difficult it is for
thofe that have attained the age of reafon and
reflection, to fupprefs the vice we fpeak of,
than for thofe to do fo, who are either children,
or have all the innocence of children.

Recollect, then, firft of all, (for you have
read, no doubt, the Acts of the Apoftles) what
was the behaviour of St. Paul when heard by
Ananias and the council at Jerufalem. This
Ananias, we muft let you know, was then
high prieft, and, confequently, one of very
great authority among the Jews. Before this
Ananias, Paul was brought to anfwer on an
accufa-

accufation of his countrymen for ftirring up the
people, but beginning his dilcourfe in fuch a
way as Ananias thought improper, he commanded thofe then ftanding clofe by Paul, to
fmite him on the mouth: on which the apoftle,
full of indignation, (for his words imply no
lefs), made anfwer, calling Ananias firft a
whited wall, which term, as a reproach, may
very eafily be underftood, and faying, " God
" hereafter fhould fmite *him* for fitting down
" to judge a man by law, and bidding him be
" fmit againft all law." Though Ananias had
put off the judge by ordering fuch an act of violence as that of fmiting an unhappy man, for
fuch the law confiders every one accufed before a judge, this conduct of the prifoner certainly was very blameable, and he confeffed as
much in his reply to thofe who afked, " if he
" reviled in fuch a manner God's high prieft ?"
when he affured them that it did not ftrike him
at the moment he had fpoke thofe words, that
Ananias was in that high place, for " I ac-
" knowledge," faid the apoftle, " we are or-
" dered not to curfe our ruler," or, as Paul
expreffed it, not fpeak evil of him. Now we
fay that Paul, in his firft anfwer, yielded to the
workings of his wrath, and erred againft his

own

own advice to the Ephesians, when he said, *be angry without sin*. Ah, little friends, this Paul had not been, from his youth, brought up in what he calls himself the nurture of the Lord, together with his admonition; and on that account discovered, to his cost, how difficult, it must be owned, to shun all provocations, as he says, to wrath.

But on that dreadful night, when Jesus was betrayed and dragged before the then high priest, what lesson have we in his conduct on this article of wrath? An officer *did* smite him, in reality, for certain words which he was pleased to fancy disrespectful, while, in Paul's affair, it was but a *command* to smite the apostle: and again, the indignity proceeded then from Ananias, the high priest, whereas, in this case, a mere subaltern, or one whom, very possibly, we should distinguish by a name of great contempt, was guilty of the violence. What, then, did Jesus Christ proceed to? Did he call the officer a *whited wall?* or beg of God to smite off the audacious hand that had presumed to lift itself against him? Far, far otherwise! Hear it attentively, good children, and then ask yourselves, if you, so treated, would have shown yourselves so patient? *If*, said Jesus, *I*

spoke

*fpoke evil, witnefs it againft me: but if well,
why haft thou fmitten me?* And did the Son of
God fay this? He whom his father would
have aided with a hoft of angels, had he prayed
for fuch affiftance? But in Jefus' breaft was
that fimplicity and innocence with which there
can be nothing upon earth in any manner worthy of comparifon, but the fimplicity and innocence of children.

Thefe are thofe two fketches we defigned to
give you. May the laft, dear little ones, particularly dwell within your minds, and, taught
by fo divine a model, may you never think it
glorious to determine on revenge, when you
are injured or infulted: rather, may God's
grace inftruct you how much more heroical,
as well as how much more contributory to your
peace, it muft be, upon all occafions, to fupprefs that anger, which can never be indulged
in, without fin. And may you finally reflect,
that David, fparing Saul, was greater in God's
eye than David trampling on Goliath, fince,
in one cafe, he might be conceived as giving
way to the emotions of his anger, and fubdu-
ing, by mere ftrength, a *man*; but, in the
other, as poffeffing his whole foul in peace,
and vanquifhing, by the affiftance of God's

grace,

grace, *himself*, fo too, dear lovely little ones, may you, in every circumftance of life, when others would perhaps give way, at leaft, to an impatient, peevifh difpofition, and be conquered by their wrath—may you, we fay, inftructed by Chrift Jefus's example, *ftruggle to obtain that much more glorious conqueft of yourfelves.* So be it, in the name of God, to whom, &c.

THE HYMN,

HOW unbecoming is the fight,
When children, who fhould fhrink with fright
If angry menaces they hear,
Angry, themfelves, too oft' appear!

Whene'er this anger clouds the face,
Of its wont charms no fign we trace:
Vanifh its colours, and in lieu
Reigns a deep fire, or death-like hue.

Our limbs too, which God's hand has made,
In comely act to be difplay'd,
If furious wrath the breaft dilate,
Convulfive motions agitate.

Let

Let no fuch favage tyrant, then,
Which finks to beafts the fons of men,
Poffefs our hearts, that ne'er fhould know
The rage of any inbred foe.

But in the fpirit of God's peace,
Which bids all jarring difcord ceafe,
May we be friendly to mankind,
And ferve him with a quiet mind.

SERMON

SERMON XXXIV.

ON IMPROPER MARRIAGES.

GENESIS II. V. 18.

And the Lord God faid · it is not good that the man fhould be alone. I will make him a help meet for him.

THUS early was the focial character in man, that is to fay, a difpofition formed for company, declared by God himfelf, who having fafhioned our firft father, found it, as he fays, not good that he fhould be alone, on which, by the exertion of his power, that could do every thing, he caft him into what is called a trance, and taking out a rib from his left fide, as fome imagine, made a human creature of it, which when brought to Adam, he called woman; faying " fhe is bone extracted from my bone, " and flefh created of my flefh, on which ac- " count," remarks, the hiftorian, namely Mofes, " fhall a man forfake his parents, and cleave

" folely to his wife, and they fhall be one
" flefh."

Do you confider this expreffion, little company? there is not one here prefent, underftanding
what is faid in common talk, but may receive
improvement from this exhortation, though undoubtedly it recommends itfelf with more propriety to fuch as are of fome years ftanding in
the world, or nearly of an age, when by the
courfe of nature they begin to have reflection,
and can reafon upon what they fee, or know
what confequences will enfue from caufes.
Give attention, therefore, fuch among you as
come under this defcription, and enabled as you
are to argue upon confequences, fhow your
judgment in a point of fo much moment to
your future peace, as the connection you may
make at prefent with an individual, who, fuppofing providence fhall fpare you to old age, you
wifh may be the partner of your life, in every
ftage thereof, in health, and ficknefs, till the
time when that old age arrives.

Confider, in the firft place then, that God,
as fays a certain author, did, in that production
of the woman we have mentioned, put himfelf
to the expence, if we may fo exprefs it, of a
miracle or wonder rather than have Adam left
alone.

alone. So ftrongly does the bond of nature draw us to admire the other fex, and feek true happinefs in their fociety, that Adam, we may eafily imagine, found even paradife itfelf, no paradife without a help-mate. This we may infer from our own feelings. Let not this remark however fill thofe little fair ones, that may hear us fay fo, with conceit, as if their fex alone had the exclufive privilege of waking admiration, and affording happinefs, as in the ftile of modern gallantry, or what is called good breeding, they are faid to do. The privilege is held in common by both fexes, and however affectation may difguife the matter, men undoubtedly are *no lefs capable than women of* awaking admiration, and affording happinefs. And therefore had it been God's pleafure to create the woman firft, his providence would doubtlefs have confidered it not good that *fhe* fhould be alone. We thought it needful to premife thus much, that thofe among the gentler fex, who are our hearers, might at leaft on one occafion hear that truth to which they will be generally fpeaking, ftrangers, and exactly know their real confequence. From fuch a knowledge they will draw improvement, and refpect themfelves, but the enormous flatttery,

with

with which they are befieged by men of modern
manners, is a fnare that often proves their ruin,
for fuppofe a little beauty were addreffed by
one who, as the phrafe is, may defire to court
her, in thefe terms : " my dear, dear angel ' you
" were born to make me happy ! Heaven is in
" your arms ! your beauty is a prefent which
" the Gods muft envy mortals, and my happi-
" nefs is greater far than theirs ! your fmile
" alone may make me bleffed ! your frown
" would drive me to defpair !" Suppofe,
we fay, fuch language that of courtfhip, as it
is, and then fuppofe the perfon fo addreffed
confents to make her flatterer happy, as he
fays fhe will, by marrying him, what wife is
fuch a perfon likely to become ? Will fhe who
has been praifed in this egregious manner,
prove the better for fuch adulation ? And ftill
more, if fhe have children ; (for to thofe dear
objects, as to pledges of their happinefs, all people marrying univerfally look forward ,) is it
likely that a mother, who has been thus flattered,
will direct her care in fuch a manner as fhe
fhould do, nay in *any* manner, to the virtuous
education of thofe children ? Is it probable
that fhe will teach them to lift up their little hands
to heaven, and contemplate on their creator

there,

there, as foon as they have underftanding to
conceive they could not make themfelves? Will
fhe do this who has been told fhe is herfelf an
angel, born on purpofe to make others happy?
She will think fhe is herfelf the happinefs of
thofe proceeding from her. Will fhe think it
neceffary to direct them in what words they
ought to pray? She is herfelf that heaven to
which they fhould direct their homage; for
her hufband frequently has told her, heaven is
in her arms. Will fhe, fuppreffing, or elfe
turning to blot out, a falling tear, defire that
God would give them every one a feeling heart?
From heaven (for fhe can underftand no other
by the Gods her hufband fpoke of) did herfelf
come to him as a prefent, and her fojourn-
ment among mankind, occafions envy in the
heart of that divinity who dwells in heaven,
while the poffeffion of her beauty renders him,
who has fucceeded to her bed, much happier
than even God himfelf Will fhe correct them?
Will fhe beg that the Almighty, in his grace,
would make them docile to his infpirations?
She has heard, and heard it too from one whom
fhe can perfectly rely on, that her fmile alone
can make beholders bleffed, and that her
frown will drive them to defpair. Once more,

M 3   we

we fay, dear children, is it likely that a bride,
thus flattered, fhould become a valuable wife?
The anfwer to this queftion we confider it unneceffary to detail you,—Artemifia may fupply it.—(Artemifia let me call you, for the
forrows you have undergone, within the pale
of your own family, are certainly enough, nor
need you be expofed by name to public obfervation)—Flattered, in the time of youth, by
him you married to, you were not anxious to
beftow upon that lovely family you brought
into the world, a virtuous education ; being half
perfuaded you fhould be the godlefs of their
worfhip or idolatry, as previoufly to that unhappy marriage you contracted with your hufband, he had faid would be the cafe. This
flattery he dealt in to obtain poffeffion of your
fortune, an *obfequious* lover then, but now,
employed, as he appears, in diffipating what
you gave him, a *tyrannic* hufband. What,
then, is the confequence of this preceding adulation? Shall we tell our little hearers?—
Your large family, of which the eldeft is at prefent grown to manhood, never having had religious precepts or examples fet before them, are
at prefent, every one among them in fucceffion,
as he grows to years of what is called reflection,

tion, finking into vice.   A loathfome malady,
or bodily diforder, caufed by what fome people, from miftake call love, and not deducible
fiom heirfhip, (for, with all your faults, this
bodily difoider ran not in your veins) from day
to day gains ground upon their tender limbs;
and long before they can obtain that property,
which, at the time they were not in the world,
was vefted in the hands of others foi thein benefit, and which you cannot, if you would,
confume, they aie themfelves confuming, by
the aid of ufurers and thieves.   You fee, too
late, the ruin of your hopes, which were as
fair as any other woman's, and feem feelingly
convinced you are not the divinity youi hufband faid you weie, becaufe he knew you
would believe him.   Let your fortune be a leffon in the ear of thofe we pieach to, and convince them that a bride, as we have faid juft
now, fo flatteied, never can become a valuable
wife.

How more ingenuoufly does not Solomon
make mention of your fex, dear children? And
what greater compliment not pay you? Could
his character of what he calls a virtuous woman be derived from the defcription of her lovers, in fuch cafe the language that at prefent

M 4   makes

makes up courtſhip, would not be the language
of deceit, and women would, when wives, in
every view be better for the vows, when they
were virgins, paid them, nor would Solomon
have left it upon record, that a virtuous woman's price exceeds, by far, the worth of ru-
bies, they would be more plenteous. Hear,
then, how king Solomon deſcribes a worthy
woman. You may find what we allude to in
the one and thirtieth chapter of his Proverbs,
verſe the 10th, &c. to the end. " Her huſ-
" band's heart," he ſays, " truſts in her. She
" will do him good, while living, and not evil.
" She is up before the day commences, and
" diſtributes meat to all that are her ſervants.
" She delights to uſe her needle, and is occu
" pied in ſpinning. She relieves the poor,
" and ſtretcheth forth her hands to all the
" needy. Silk and purple is her raiment. By
" the labour of her hands does ſhe array her
" huſband, who is known among the nobles
" from the elegance of his apparel. Her own
" clothing is no leſs than ſtrength and honour.
" Wiſdom iſſues from her lips, and kindneſs
" ſits upon her tongue She looketh carefully
" to what her houſehold are employed in, and
" will never eat the bread of idleneſs. Her
                                                " children

" children blefs her, and that hufband praifes
" her œconomy and virtue, who has been fo
" fortunate as to obtain her."

Such is the defcription of a virtuous woman:
but before the author of the Proverbs gives it,
he enquires where fuch a one is to be found?
which is as much as if he had informed us fuch
a character is very fcarce · but wherefore fo?
Is it in fome fort neceffary that the female character fhould be exceptionable? Oh, not fo!
By nature, and the will of providence, a woman is entirely the reverfe, and, making fome
fmall change in what the poet fays, we may
addrefs ourfelves in their behalf to Virtue,
with the apoftrophe of *Virtue, thy true name is
Woman.* But why, then, does vice fo frequently ufurp their likenefs? Why, dear children, but becaufe the breath of flattery, from
the time of childhood, undermines their lovelinefs, and caufes that fome cenfurers, in their
converfation and their books, fo frequently
launch out into invectives, like the following:
Vanity, thy name is Woman. And who, pray,
conceive you, are thofe cenfurers? Such as
have before hand not refufed to be the very
flatterers that have fed this vanity in thofe they
can be fo unmanly as to cenfure and upbraid.

We

We take occasion, therefore, from this observation, to address ourself to you 'that rank
among the sex called manly, if of that descrip-
tion any are here present, though, if not, the
advice will be of use to you, dear little fair
ones; and we say, it seems to us no bad continuation of the present subject, if we warn
you never to insult the modesty and understanding of that individual you may very likely have
selected from among the other sex, with nause-
ous praises on her person, such as she must
know she has no claim to. Never let such
charms as those of Venus, and the Graces, be
appropriated to *your charmer*, when you court
her. Surely she will have enough to please
you, if her air and gesture, attitude, appearance,
and deportment be as beautiful as nature or
God's providence designed to make them.
They, who by their suitors have been praised
as goddesses before they married, always prove
much less than women after. The civilities of
life, indeed, require we should adopt the language of politeness, and this language is a coin
that will do well enough for those who meet
perhaps to-day, and on the morrow will not
see each other, but the style of courtship, that
we mean, which should be had recourse to by

two

two perfons that have hopes of fpending their whole lives together, and be fellow fharers of that happinefs which either of them fhall attain to, fhould be built upon the bafis of ftrict truth. If, as in common life we own is frequently the cafe, it fhould make either of two lovers hate the other, what is to be faid, but that the hated perfon luckily has trod upon a ferpent in the grafs, and which has therefore bit his *leg:* he might have flept upon the fpot, and in the midft of golden dreams been bitten to the *heart.* In fhort, the fum of our advice upon the matter, little hearers, may be comprehended in the following maxim: namely, that provided any of you, either male or female, cultivate a friendfhip with the perfon you defire to marry, you would act, not only wickedly but inconfiftently, if you fhould go about to funder your expreffion from your thoughts. On fuch occafions more particularly is the proverb verified, that honefty muft be, for ever, the beft policy.

To thefe inftructions, on the choice of a connection, fuch as is moft likely to affect your happinefs, we add another, namely, the advice of thofe who are entitled to expect you will folicit it, and *that* before you fet your heart

upon

upon the object you conceive you may approve
of, and before you drop a hint to any one but
them upon the bufinefs. They may, very likely,
have to ftart one grand objection, which your
inexperience and precipitation to be happy,
will not let you think of, even granting that
in point of morals you have pitched upon a
proper perfon. That one grand objection is,
difparity or inequality of fortune, fince unequal
matches frequently are fatal to both parties,
but of all difparity, or inequality, an inequality
in point of education muft eventually be unhappy. After this, dear children, let not any
one among you wonder that fo many admoni-
tions are effential on a point of fuch import-
ance, but defire of God, that as you grow
in years, you may advance in reafon, to difcern the truth of what we have been preaching
to you. " Oh great God," fay every night,
at leaft, and morning to him, when you thank
his mercy for the bleffings of the cheerful day,
and fupplicate him to protect you from the
danger of the night, " be gracious to us, and
" vouchfafe that we may rather be preferved in
" the fimplicity and innocence peculiar to our
" youth, than lofe it though we afterwards
" repent, and that we may obtain this happi-
" nefs,

" nefs, oh keep us in the obfervation of thofe
" various duties we already have fufficient un-
" derftanding to be fenfible are laid upon us,
" and of which the chief is unconditional obe-
" dience to our parents, who know better
" what is fitting for us than ourfelves ; but,
" more than all, let thy good providence pre-
" ferve us from the unhappinefs which fuch
" connections as they know will be improper,
" muft bring down upon our heads.   Give us,
" in fhort, the grace to be convinced that every
" blefling is comprifed in *that* which thou haft
" pledged thy promife to beftow on fuch as
" honour, as they ought, their parents.   Then
" will this aurora of our life be followed by a
" fplendid day.   The bloffom of our childhood
" will produce ripe fruit when we are grown
" to men and women.   We fhall now be
" bleffed with pleafure, and in time reap wif-
" dom.   Finally, becaufe at prefent we evince
" the prudence of obedience, we fhall be here-
" after happy in the crown thou wilt beftow
" on all thy children, when this world is done
" away, and thy eternal reign begins.   Hear
" us, we pray thee, for the fake of Jefus
" Chrift, to whom, as well as to the Holy
" Spirit, be afcribed all praife, dominion, ma-
jefty,

" jefty, and might, now, henceforth, and for
" evermore. Amen."

THE HYMN.

MARRIAGE is a ferious thing!
Let me enter, Lord, therein,
Not as numbers round me do,
Foolifhly and rafhly too:
    Every day
  Thefe fore-fraught,
    Dearly pay
For their folly or their fault.

Of the rougher fex if born,
Let me Flattery's language fcorn;
Nor a goddefs, when I wooe,
Title her to whom I fue.
    Sure for me,
  All I need
    Muft it be,
If fhe prove what God decreed.

                    And

And if female I am made,
Be my reafon more difplay'd
Than my fuitor to believe,
Flattering fo a child of Eve.
  Sure for me,
 All I need
  Muft it be,
If I prove what God decreed,

END OF VOLUME II,

CPSIA information can be obtained at www.ICGtesting.com
Printed in the USA
LVOW050137200212

269462LV00003B/26/P

9 781140 723981